Tales from the Irish Club

Tales from the Irish Club

♣

A Collection of Short
Stories by
Lester Goran

The Kent State University Press
KENT, OHIO, & LONDON, ENGLAND

© 1996 by Lester Goran
All rights reserved
Library of Congress Catalog Card Number 95-37386
ISBN 0-87338-539-X
Manufactured in the United States of America

02 01 00 99 98 97 96   5 4 3 2

Designed and composed in Adobe Garamond
by Will Underwood at The Kent State University Press.
Printed by Thomson-Shore, Inc.

Library of Congress Cataloging-in-Publication Data
Goran, Lester.
Tales from the Irish Club : a collection of short stories /
by Lester Goran.
p.   cm.
ISBN 0-87338-539-X (pbk. : alk. paper) ∞
1. Irish Americans—Pennsylvania—Pittsburgh—Societies and clubs—
Fiction. 2. Pittsburgh (Pa.)—Social life and customs—Fiction.
3. Jewish men—Pennsylvania—Pittsburgh—Fiction.
I. Title.
PS3557.063T35   1996
813'.54—dc20   95-37386

British Library Cataloging-in-Publication data are available.

For Deedee

With thanks for everything to
James T., Gene C., and the late Regis Connors

Joxer: "Didja ever rade *Elizabeth, or Th' Exile o' Sibayria*
         . . . oh, it's a darlin' story, a daarlin' story!"

Boyle: "You eat your sassige, an' never min' *Th' Exile o' Sibayria.*"

—Sean O'Casey, *Juno and the Paycock,* Act I

Contents

Introduction   xi

PART ONE: *First There's Life*

1. The Other Thing   3
2. Now That Maureen's Thirty   15
3. Mortality   25

PART TWO: *Special Types*

4. The Last Visit   43
5. A Mystery   67

PART THREE: *Local Irregularities*

6. A Girl like Sheila   77
7. The Payment   85
8. Remember Me to Katie   97

PART FOUR: *Boys in the Age of Miracles*

9. The Madonna of the Jukebox   107
10. Grady's Sister   117
11. The Road to Damascus   125

Introduction

To the people living in 1965, Catholics and all, manners and ways of thinking about things seemed eternal—caught in a time of long, slow twilight, lit in the rose and gold of certainty and things in place. What was good then was comfort in the familiar, trust in institutions, no sense of an impending falling away of the customary; but the truthful heart remembering the time at its best must also affirm that, there being human beings abroad, it was not an orderly time. I do not know when the Ancient Order of Hibernians, Local No. 9, opened its doors in the second-floor loft on Oakland Avenue, but they closed in 1965, the year of the Second Vatican Council. None of us who went to the Irish Club daily, weekly, holidays like St. Patrick's Day, and every-day-a-holiday knew we were living at the end of a period of time as gone now as the Weimar Republic or the Soviet Union. Not as encompassing in numbers, geography, or issues of life and death, but we had only one time and that was it, mounting those steps, listening to the music of each other's voices, descending again befumed to play at things in place. Some of the Irish boys and the rest went to wars and did not return. Their names made a long list on the roll in the foyer of St. Agnes's Church, where their mothers, fathers, sisters, cousins, aunts, uncles, and neighbors prayed. The dead boys forgotten in their way, the living lost in theirs. No one except a fiction writer would want to perpetuate a cast of all the unremembered delegates from an abandoned time.

Whatever we thought, we were auditioning to be misplaced by history. Less recorded than Weimar. What writer, though, does not presume to speak for the forgotten? Chekhov said it should be his main business. Otherwise, what need at all for writers to give testimony if the true and simple soul can speak for itself?

PART ONE

First There's Life

ONE

The Other Thing

IT WAS to young Farley's credit that he could fit in anywhere, but as his mother confided to Mrs. Condon one night in 1954, it was no great accomplishment because he never fit in anyplace anybody much would want to belong. Not that anyone in the Farley family had achieved anything else much better that anyone would have envied. The elder Farley brother was a postman who had been convicted of throwing first-class mail into a sewer and sentenced to two years at Blaw Knox. The father died early of pneumonia, and a sister disappeared one week in April 1951 and was never mentioned and hardly remembered, except by her mother. Young Farley had only his mother to please, and Mrs. Farley—no optimist by life's experience—expected very little: to attend the Irish Club in happy times and on holidays, an occasional Saturday, staring when she was alone into the rainbows of the jukebox-lit night for images of her boys, who had been boys like any others. She searched too for the daughter, who had not seemed the sort to bolt and fly from her own life to Denver or Seattle or maybe Philadelphia without a postcard. There danced in the amberglow not quite clearly her husband, hardly an adventurous sort, a mill worker. But he'd hopped into eternity, brisk, young, and eager like a man who had chosen frail health and the unknown boldly. He went at thirty-seven, leaving her young Farley—Johnny—who was well liked but never made a living, held a job longer than three months, or could stand out in a crowd of ten men, or two for that matter.

Johnny, however, had a remarkable notion while he was a child, perhaps ten or eleven, and sat in the classes at St. Agnes. It came to him one day while he listened to one of the sisters talk of various saints who had been called to love in strange ways, ways peculiar to people who understand neither God nor sainthood. He wondered as he listened whether he would receive such a call, and with time realized he wouldn't, scarcely understanding where to look for it or how. But he knew with certainty that he would one day do what he thought of as "the other thing." It would be something other people would admire, notice him for, talk about. He looked for it all through parochial school, then Schenley High, where he dropped out in the ninth grade. He decided it would be long in coming but sure and he would know it when it finally came.

He stored the idea away like a squirrel putting away an acorn in a large dead tree and seldom over the years brought it out to look at it, to turn it over in his mind. Sometimes he forgot it for months, its strange promise, sometimes for years at a time, despite its certainty to him.

Johnny stood around on corners as he grew to manhood and was not attentive to his mother. He would help her carry packages up from the Giant Eagle on Forbes but never watched television with her or accompanied her to Mass or the occasional wedding. He left her to the company of Mrs. Condon, a widow from around the corner on Terrace, or Mrs. Noonan, another widow, whose son was the invisible man too at their home on Dunseith. The three widows often gathered at one another's houses and drank a beer or two. They wondered aloud why fate had chosen some women to be grandmothers of seventeen or even thirty grandchildren and other women to lie abed at uncertain hours of the night and wonder where their husbands' souls might be at that moment and when their wandering sons or daughters yet confined to earth would come through the door to the porch downstairs, tiptoeing in the darkness of the parlor. Some of the living would never return: Mrs. Farley's daughter was named Virginia, and Mrs. Farley missed her dreadfully by the hour, even the minute; and young Johnny was no consolation. Johnny leaned in doorways on street corners with his shirttail out and his collar turned up or his sleeves rolled high on his arms, and when a tide of boys was swept by some mysterious impulse up Forbes to the park, Johnny went with them in a merry pack, shouting and singing as they strode purposefully to a park bench or the entrance to the University Tavern. When the same wind of another destination blew them elsewhere, in their midst Johnny would go too, back to the same corner where the evening had begun.

On these street forays, without a job, earning a pittance as an usher on an infrequent weekend at Forbes Field selling pennants and popcorn, Johnny Farley grew to twenty-three years of age—stocky, never quite combed, his clothes unpressed, a burden to his mother—and then he married. His new wife was a young woman named Sissie Collins, whose brother was Chips Collins, a longtime friend of Johnny's, who had enlisted in the Coast Guard in the early 1950s and then had reenlisted.

Sissie Collins had a job as a waitress at the Mandarin Village Restaurant, where she worked the lunch and dinner hours, receiving in addition to her salary and tips two meals a day. After she and Johnny were married, living at her parents' house on Bates Street, near the boulevard, she made it a condition of her employment that Johnny be given two meals a day there too. Arthur Cheng, the Chinese cook who also owned the restaurant—and had since before the war in Europe—found Sissie an excellent waitress, and while he did not like Johnny's looks, agreed to two meals a day for Johnny for most of the week but not on Saturday or Sunday nights, when the Mandarin Village attracted families out for dinner. Johnny ate with Sissie every day, killing time between meals as he usually did, until Sissie was done for the evening, and then the two of them at ten walked down to Bates. She worked seven days a week because the salary was small and the tips were mostly what they lived on.

Johnny had never been happier, and Sissie, a tall girl with long thin legs and a face pale as venetian blinds, began to achieve color in her cheeks, and her eyes, always striking, shifted from green to blue in pleasure when she looked at her new husband. At nights Johnny was a familiar figure leaning in the doorway across the street from the Mandarin Village—the cook asked him once a month not to block his entrance—waiting for Sissie. In rain and snow and fine nights with the stars bright over Pittsburgh, they walked home the mile to Bates Street, laughing, talking, holding hands, and on Saturday nights at midnight, they came to the Irish Club and danced.

In time Sissie had a baby, a daughter, and she took ten days off from work and she and Johnny tended the baby. Johnny's mother came to visit once a day, walking quickly the mile down to Bates but with joy in her stride, her small purse clutched to her side to avoid theft. She had never been robbed, but she knew that behind the most innocent appearances lay the greatest evils. She delighted in the baby and would have gladly seen to it every day, but between Sissie's mother and Johnny she felt unnecessary and stopped coming once a day. It turned out Johnny was very good with his daughter, giving up loitering on Forbes and in the park, seldom leaving the house to run with his friends. He spent his days with the child, whose name was Sharon. When she was two months old, Johnny carried her up to the Mandarin Village and held her while he ate his Chinese food, and Arthur Cheng, who considered Johnny no better than any of the street boys he put out occasionally for noise or roughhousing, said nothing when Johnny brought with him too the baby every day to eat Chinese food. Johnny now woke early before Sissie and fed the baby, then brought Sissie her breakfast, and usually walked with her and Sharon to the Mandarin Village to see Sissie off to work. He returned for lunch with Sharon, took her home for her nap, and came back for dinner. At ten at night he waited with the baby across the street from the restaurant, and as in the old days, rain or shine, he accompanied Sissie back home down to Bates, telling her events of the day and what Sharon had done. Sharon grew into a high chair at the Mandarin Village and then began to walk quite well, a small child balanced on sturdy legs like Johnny's, rather than Sissie's stilts. Johnny thought himself never happier and told his mother so when he brought Sharon to visit her on Sundays after noon Mass, while Sissie worked, and told Chips Collins the same when he came home for a long furlough in 1958.

"I have everything I need," Johnny said. "I never thought things were going to turn out this good. You know, Sissie is one wife in a million. She never complains, no ache and pains and all that, works every day, and she's happy as me. She doesn't care about the little things in raising Sharon, and since I'm around most of the time I can keep an eye on Sharon and it's best for everyone."

"I don't know, Johnny," Chips said. When Chips came home he took his old room and slept there with Sharon and didn't mind. He said listening to the child breathing was better music to fall asleep to than the sounds of his mates sawing logs all night. "There's something not right about it," Chips added, having done well in the service.

"It's not permanent," Johnny said. "I have an application in to the Pittsburgh Hotel downtown and the William Penn. Bellboys get rich if they have the right location, but you know, those guys hold on to the job until they're carried out like a suitcase. Someone shouts, 'Boy!' and there comes up a little sixty-two-year-old man to carry your bag. But I'm versatile. I don't need to go into one line of work. I went down to the barber college and I looked around and I'm considering it. And there's a place gives you a three-week course in floral arrangement I'm thinking over. A fellow owning his own flower shop gets a Cadillac with his third bunch of roses he puts together, the money they charge. I haven't been sitting here. I know one thing, I'm not going into Jones and Laughlin like the old man.

It's what killed him at an early age. I'm not committing suicide with what I have going for me."

Sissie agreed and said there was no hurry. With what she'd have to pay someone to take care of Sharon, her mother not well enough to chase a little kid, they were saving money with Johnny tending the child. Chips was not one to question other people's happiness; he inquired no further.

Johnny's luck continued. Watching a card game one afternoon at the Meyron Avenue Public School, he heard that the maintenance man who allowed the game in his small room off the furnace was quitting. Johnny moved closer. The man's name was Joe Brandt, an old-timer who had been friends with his father. "Mr. Brandt," Johnny said, quick to sense an opportunity, "I'd appreciate it if you'd put in a word for me. This would be my cup of tea. I'd make you proud, keep things like you always did. Meyron Avenue would stay a showplace as if you were still running it. Mention me to the boss, okay?"

In two weeks, after the interview with Mr. Cardiff, the principal, and Mrs. Sheffman, the assistant principal in charge of buildings and grounds, Johnny was hired. He had all to himself the tending of the furnace, supervising the painting of the gym floors, the broken locks in the students' locker rooms, and the fine graft of ten dollars the cardplayers gave him weekly to come in after four when the school was closed and the fiver neighborhood sheiks paid him now and again for the use of the janitor's room when, as they said, "Your William Penn downtown is booked solid." Money, love of the schoolkids, neighborhood people all greeting him by name as he came to work, and best, still within walking distance to take Sharon up for lunch and dinner with Sissie at the Mandarin Village—it was a time good to be alive, but Johnny knew the other thing had not come to pass, even as men with whom he had not been friendly, particularly a fellow named Finn Mooney, now nodded at him at his card games and called to him by name. Johnny was not yet as welcomed or admired as in the dreamglow once the new time began.

"Say, Johnny," Finn said, after twenty years of silence, "you look like that uniform was made for you." Young Farley wore a blue uniform with the word *Johnny* in a circle stitched on by Sissie at the breast. Johnny had known Finn since they both attended St. Agnes, but they did not live on the same street. Finn lived on a parallel street leading up to the top of the hill, Dunseith. Finn studied Johnny, sometimes turning away when Johnny looked back at him, other times directly looking at him, and then when he married Sissie, looking too long at her too at the Irish Club, but never as intently as he looked at Johnny. From boyhood on, Finn scrutinized him, and Johnny thought Finn would speak to him one day of something that bothered him about Johnny. But Finn never spoke. They did not say hello to each other, and Johnny had been troubled. No one singled him out to look at, or Johnny thought, to think about much. He blended into crowds, was hardly observed as he stood in doorways. One night he had taken the microphone at the Irish Club and sung "My Wild Irish Rose" and people stood and cheered, but two days later no one mentioned it to him, and a week later, bringing it up himself, no one remembered the singer or the song. He had not known what to do about Finn Mooney's unblinking concern with him.

Some people said Finn was crazy and secretive, and Johnny worried about himself and Sissie and the baby. No one knew Finn well. Once he had wrestled a brother to the ground in an argument in a soccer game. He was a muscular young man who wore tight shirts and worked on the loading docks at the Pennsylvania and Lake Erie Railroad. His features were regular, his expression was untroubled, and he had a smooth pale skin. But when other people laughed at a joke about a woman's folly, a drunkard, or a memorable moment, Finn sneered as if he had caught either the storyteller or the subject in a discreditable error. He smiled but never laughed. He seemed to regard the world as foolish, hardly able to contain his contempt, and he usually drank alone at the bar of whatever tavern he visited, even at the Irish Club, usually leaving at eleven, busy, off on more important adventures. It was said he ran nightly to the whorehouses on the North Side, but no one had ever seen him there. He was never seen with a woman, and if anything at all was noted about him, it was how intently he stared at young Farley. It had gone on so long Johnny seldom thought of it directly and decided he would never understand the matter. But now they became the greatest of friends. Still with the same almost puzzled look at Johnny sometimes, Finn occasionally came to their table at the Irish Club, spoke to him at the card games at Meyron School, even once asked Johnny if he needed a silverware set he had lifted at the P and LE loading platform. "No," Johnny said, "but it's fine you asked, Finn. I appreciate it."

"Things come up now and then," Finn said. "I'll keep you in mind." Johnny felt a final joy lay just beyond his grasp; tantalized, he could not put it into words. "I knew something good was going to happen to me one day," Johnny said. "It's in my cards. I knew it from a kid. Old Finn, he never spoke, it shows you: I thought it was something bad, it was just his way." Now they had enough money to give Sissie's cousin, a young girl named Caitlin, a small amount to come in on weekdays and look after Sharon. At the kitchen table they figured out their finances: it was May, and by July there'd be enough to take a place of their own, and by the end of the year there'd be enough to look for a house. Johnny took his little girl to the park in the summer and they played on the swings and slides, and at night he and Sissie called on Caitlin and went up to the Irish Club, even on weekdays. Johnny waited. Was the school going to burn and Johnny Farley save fourteen young lives?

In the last days of summer, before the new semester started at Meyron in 1960, Johnny met Finn one day while he stood in front of the bank looking for Sissie to finish work at ten. From his doorway across the street from the Mandarin Village, Johnny hailed Finn. He had left Sharon at home, and there was plenty of time before Sissie finished work. Johnny enjoyed loitering. He thought of Sissie in her apron across the street and wondered about his lost sister and his brother. Even before Sharon and his new job, he liked to lean in the doorway watching people pass and saying hello to friends. He liked being known. Happy with his new friendship, Johnny went to have a beer with Finn down at Coyne's a block away. They drank until it was too late to meet Sissie, but Johnny knew she'd understand. Sometimes it happened that way: then later at night, as if they had been separated for weeks, he'd slide into bed beside her late and beery and they would embrace tender and hard, and all night long. Finn and Johnny drank until Coyne's closed at two and both of them were staggering. It had been a good night. Finn's memory of places in their youth was like Johnny's, exact and complete, and they both laughed over clowns they had known and good people who had died too early.

At about two-thirty they decided to pitch pennies, as boys used to when they met on Robinson or Dunseith, the one whose penny came closest to the wall the winner. Forbes was quiet, the summer night a warm wind that came and went blowing a *Post-Gazette* in tatters before it. Only an occasional streetcar's clang sounded on the long, hollow street. Johnny was well ahead when Finn began to argue about each call, plainly wrong. They threw their pennies against the wall of the Sea Breeze Beauty Supply Store. Inside the dark window, mannequins' heads sat bald and rounder than a human being's. "Okay," Johnny agreed each time, not wishing to argue, even hoping Finn could catch up and then they'd quit.

Finn turned after a loss of three straight tosses and seized Johnny by the collar. "I could kill you," Finn said.

"Don't," Johnny said. "Let's stop now."

"I always could," Finn said. "I knew it when I first saw you. I knew I could kill you. I never knew what stopped me."

Johnny wasn't afraid. He took Finn's wrist. "Let go, Finn," he said.

Before him Finn rose like a street wind gone mad, with roofs flying before it, in roars like a freight train, large and unstoppable; "Oh God," Johnny said, already fighting, but knowing nothing in Oakland could stop the frenzy that had blown down suddenly on Johnny Farley from up on Robinson, now husband, father, good son. Breathing hard, Finn threw Johnny back, and growled, "It was already done in my mind a thousand times. It was done a thousand, thousand times." The sound Johnny heard was Finn's fists striking his face. He felt twisted by the wind, by darkness, whirled and disembodied. He clawed at Finn's wrists. But even after it had become dark and light again and Johnny had cried out, "Finn, you're killing me," he knew that Finn was still at it. It hurt and stopped and hurt again, everywhere. He felt the blows distantly and knew he lay on the sidewalk and Finn was kicking him. "Stop," he mumbled, thinking it was not happening to young Farley, but it went on. He was numb and felt no more. The thumps continued. It's my face, he thought, the blows far away and soft. It might have been another day when he became aware of the policeman who lifted him from the curb and then the emergency room of the Montefiore Hospital. "Did you see who did it?" a policeman asked, as the nurses in the hospital cut off Johnny's shirt. "It was a man named Finn Mooney," Johnny said, watching the clothes with his blood thrust into the open trap of a white wastebasket.

The police later thought he had been delirious. Seldom had a fight between two men who knew each other turned into a brain concussion, an eye almost lost—so battered the victim would have to wear a patch for months, maybe years—a shattered nose, one arm broken at the wrist and elbow, the other arm almost torn from its socket, the knees swollen to where he might never walk without a cane again. Johnny's teeth had punctured the cheeks of his face before most of them had been knocked out. "More like a street gang or a building collapse," one officer said. "This wasn't done by a person."

Johnny was not expected to live but recovered slowly, first four weeks in the hospital, then home in casts and bars. He walked about after a while with two canes and his head in bandages with a neck brace he would have to wear, the doctors said, for years. Sissie was loving as always, asking only at the beginning, "But why'd he do it?" Johnny could not answer. "We were pitching pennies," he said. "He was behind twenty-two cents."

Johnny's mother came daily, and when Johnny asked for water, his mother and wife ran to get it and gave it to Sharon to hold to his lips and he drank. The case against Finn dragged on. He said he had left Johnny asleep in a doorway and had come home when he couldn't wake him. Who had beaten him was a mystery to him. Finn sat at the bar in the Irish Club, no more frequently, no less, daring anyone to accuse him of the crime. When Johnny first came to the club a year later, after hobbling up the long stairs to the third floor, Finn approached him and said boldly, "You got it wrong, Johnny. It never happened like you think."

Johnny through one eye stared straight ahead. "I'm sorry for what happened to you," Finn said, retreating. "I had nothing to do with it." People who had hardly spoken to Johnny before sent over pitchers of beer, and he never paid for his own. Women patted Sissie's arm and said, "You're a model of courage," and Johnny's mother, at another table with Mrs. Condon, grew warm and flushed when she looked at her youngest. "You know," she told her friend, "I'll bet that assassin insulted me or members of our family and Johnny fought him like a tiger." At the school, Mr. Cardiff told him his job waited for him. Johnny sat in the center of a golden circle, people entering it to tell him he was lucky to be alive and admiring his health and courage. Inside the circle with him he was proud to make room for his failed brother, now an assistant cafeteria manager in Akron, and his sister, who had disappeared, as if a sheet had been draped on all her comings and goings for twenty-six years and she removed to a remote part of the attic where in the darkness of memory and time no one could discern the proportions of her once-being. He had, Johnny thought, allowing Sissie to hold a glass of beer to his swollen lips, at last entered the final good time and place and brought all his people. Through the eye covered by a patch, the streamers of lights over the bar and the people dancing in the long mirror looked like everything as it should be.

He could take a beating and the world knew it.

It was like the day a carnival had been held on an empty field on Ward Street. Not having the money for admission, boys stood on the edges and waited for a good thing to happen. Johnny slipped in, climbing a fence, tore apart with his bare hands rotted wooden planks and let in nine boys—free. The ferris wheel lights were spinning in his battered brain as he saw before him in the mirror his vanished sister and his father dead too young and his brother the criminal postman, all dancing.

Now That Maureen's Thirty

T HE FIRST letter came in a blue envelope. It had no return ad-
dress but it had been mailed from Pittsburgh, and it read: "You
are one in a million. You are a real lady. I would like to know you
better." It was signed, "A Gentleman."

Maureen tore it to shreds. It was, she thought, one of her brothers—she had four—or one of their friends pulling a prank on her.
Huge, hulking shapes, her brothers trudged like horses in blinders
the hill outside, up Robinson, men who might have been part of a
misty night or a sunny day, simple and pointless as whatever the
weather was like out of doors. Sometimes in dreams she saw them
dressed in yellow rain slickers advancing on her in menace as she sat
on the tiny family porch on Robinson.

Their names were Knockout, Jay, Bully, and Sid. If a young man
had come to call on her, they would have frightened him off, sitting
in their undershirts, chests matted with hair and sweat, unshaven in
the house, white stockinged feet on ottomans, and falling asleep
over lit cigarettes in their ashtrays. Her father sat at a card table in
the dining room and played solitaire, angry with his sons, Maureen,
the weather, and the state of his stiff neck. He had once been a
policeman and had been shot in the neck when he caught a burglar
on a roof, and pensioned, retired, he sat all day in an undershirt. He
hovered over cards and cursed the queen, jack, and king of spades.

He rose to go to bed at two, slept four hours, and returned to the card table.

Maureen suspected when no other letter came that the first had been sent by a man with whom she worked at Taylor Allerdyce High School in Squirrel Hill. She had been a librarian there for five years, and the man was a new assistant principal. She saw him observing her on his first day. He had taken to bringing her a cup of coffee occasionally. He said, "I envy you your way with kids. They talk to you as if you were one of them." He was a veteran of the war in the South Pacific—and unhappily married, she heard—but the truth was she did not get along with the students. They called her, just loud enough for her to catch the murmur, "Bulldog Scanlon."

Sometimes she found, torn from one of the periodicals in the library, the photograph of a dog with the words "Bulldog Scanlon" scrawled on it. At first she had held back tears; then she had let herself cry. She was short, like her brothers, and while not bunchéd in the shoulders like the other Scanlons, she had a formidable breadth for a young woman. She tried to stand straight, holding up her chin; but she knew why she was called by the odious name because she herself, no fool and not vain, thought she looked like a small, friendly bear. But her breast line was high and good, and her complexion was fresh. She liked the colors in her hair. Her hair was auburn, untouched, but glinted with an occasional copper strand, and her hands were clean and white, the fingers blunt but long. She thought of herself as well made, even sexy, but when she was thirty, the year the letter came, she had had no one thus far to confirm her own good judgment of herself. She put the letter from her mind. She arranged the periodicals, chatted with the teachers, and went to bed early, shutting the door to her room upstairs away from the noise of her brothers. She read, mostly Shelley or Keats or either of the Brownings. Outside her door she heard her brothers stumbling to bed, then at two her father climbing the steps. She could bear it: she would bear it. Life was easy for no one.

A week later another letter came. "I'm sincere," it read "and I have deep feelings for you," and it was signed again, "A Gentleman." This time she did not destroy the letter but turned it over in her hands, trying to remember whom she had told her favorite color was blue. She may have told Mr. Donegan, the assistant principal; she searched her mind for their morning conversations but she could not testify to it. In the winter session at school a third letter came, then a fourth. The letters were marked by the same reticence, the restraint of a man who did not find this path easy. He could not speak his mind fully, but he would tell her generally how the land lay. It was someone encumbered—quite possibly, someone unhappily married—too noble to break his vows, but too passionate to keep his concerns to himself.

She had Donegan's number, but each time she phoned his house, whether it was his wife or he who answered, she quickly hung up.

She received eight more letters, all in the same blue envelopes, the same honest handwriting. She put them into a bundle and tied them with a red shoelace. As the trees outside her window in the backyard bloomed in the spring of 1950, she felt connected to all that was growing, green shoots and the new shadows the warmer sun cast when she walked down Robinson.

Inside her house there was no change in season, no lifting of the sullen quiet that lay on the place. When her mother was alive, she had kept the brothers from each other. Where Maureen sought still places, wanted orderly movements and her books and records in their accustomed places, her brothers wanted disorder. They sat drinking beer in a dread quiet of hostilities mounting to confrontations. Rage overcame them all at one time or another.

They out-stared each other, brushed against each other dangerously close, and challenged each other in doorways until someone moved. She did not understand them. One had gone into her room and smashed a record of *La Traviata* she owned. None of them liked the sounds coming from her room. "Who would do something like that?" K.O. asked, shrugging his shoulders. "You broke it cleaning."

When she went to walk by herself one day, Jay, the one she had trusted most as a child, now, like the others, called: "Don't come back pregnant." Once he and she had hidden under a bush in the backyard and read lines of poetry to each other, then walked and studied sunsets on the hill behind their house before the government housing projects were built. Now he was in his thirties too, but his voice was like theirs, not hers.

"Be still!" she shouted, alarming herself with the sudden anger, and was sorry. I will not be like them, she thought. I will not.

"Don't come in after ten," Knockout, sitting on the porch, said. "This ain't an all-night hotel."

She was silent, enjoying the smells of the coming summer, the pines already sunburnt, and the well-dressed people on the street in Oakland. Fifth Avenue was like a boulevard there. Before the Syria Mosque she fell in with the crowd going to a concert. She hummed to herself.

She became convinced it was Bob Donegan. His pale, sensitive eyes followed her in the library. She felt speech trapped in him. In summer he came to her small desk on the second floor and brought her coffee and sat on the corner. Now she noticed: on some days he wore a blue suit, almost as pale as the envelopes, and a darker blue tie.

She put the letters in their blue envelopes on her desk and waited. She set them directly on an anthology of poems she kept on her desk. She knew that approaching Mr. Donegan would require stealth equal to that of a soldier slipping through barbed wire. She'd have to ensure nothing rattled and no footsteps sounded that would alarm him if he was not the sender.

He brought her in July a cup of coffee in a styrofoam cup, wearing a crisp blue suit with a blue tie, as he customarily did on Mondays. She said, "Did you have a good weekend?"

His melancholy eyes betrayed his words. She knew him. It had been terrible. His face was drawn but the old smile broke through for her; he did not want her to suffer for the youthful mistake he had made in a marriage now on the rocks. His eyes spoke in mute appeal.

"Just fine, Maureen, and you?" he said, taking his place on the edge of her desk, ready to bolt at the suggestion of imposing on her.

Can't you see, she wanted to say, I want nothing from you. I'm here to listen if you care to talk. I'm here to be sorry or sad or happy with you. I'm not here for myself; I'm here to be your friend. I don't need more. Let others make demands. Just trust me with what tears at your heart.

"I went to church," she said, "the usual."

"I went down to St. Paul's this Sunday," he said. "I haven't been there in years."

"I've been there often. We used to walk out when we were kids."

"There was a crowd. And so hot out."

"It's an experience," she said. She paused because she wanted to think of him there, to see him in the great cathedral on Fifth. Was he there with the woman who had blighted his life? Did he take his children?

"My wife slept in," he said. "Doris usually goes to late Mass. I took the children."

He had given her a picture to savor: she saw herself kneeling next to him at the communion rail, leaving the gorgeous cathedral together.

"It was a fine day for walking," she said, hoping for more pictures of the three of them out on Fifth now, blinking in the Sunday sunlight, but Mr. Donegan said, "I'd better get back before they send out a search party."

After he was gone, she looked about the library after him, sensing the air. She could not say for certain he had even observed the blue envelopes on her desk, or made a note of them. But he would not be one to give himself away that easily, a shy, subtle man. She had no friends with whom she could discuss her admirer. Bringing anyone to her house was impossible. When she was young, she had accepted no invitations. Not that any came lately.

Knowing that she would never be mistaken for a lady on the cover of *Photoplay* anyhow, she nightly dressed like a queen on parade—filled with expectation and a movement inside her that made her lose the power of speech, maybe it was love—and presented herself to the rich streets of Oakland. She avoided looking into the low, drinking man's bars on Forbes, took herself instead out to the sumptuous Schenley Hotel. Without the courage just yet to walk up to the wide veranda that ran under a canopy the length of the building on Forbes and Bellefield, she paced the street outside the hotel as nights fell.

A stranger, she thought, would think her a woman from the fine assortment who stayed at the Schenley. And Donegan, no stranger, perhaps observing her in the summer dusk, would understand each gesture, every sway to her that meant love waited in her like a tiger snarling at the bars to the cage of her long, hot days.

Pulling her nerve together, on a Friday she boldly took the Fifth Avenue stairs up to the veranda. She walked between the outside tables as if she searched for a friend. This is the moment for your announcement, she thought. Come, Donegan.

Men looked. No one spoke.

She went inside to the Hunt Room and took a stool at the bar. She ordered a Tom Collins. She looked neither to right nor to left. She gazed inward.

At a far corner of the bar, several men were laughing among themselves. They wore summer suits of cord and pale, lineny material. She heard the words "Minnesota" and "Minneapolis." She did not look up, but she smiled when they laughed. She felt friendship for everyone in the bar and not at all alone.

Would he come through the door at this moment, having allowed her to settle herself?

No customers sat between Maureen and the men grouped at the other end of the bar. That was the point about getting out into the world: ten minutes from her house on Robinson, and she could sit among people from all corners of the United States. A convention, salesmen, teachers, people who traveled and saw things and knew what was what.

Donegan, you fill my heart with belonging.

"Have you ever been to Minnesota?" one of the men called to her.

Maureen shook her head no.

The man walked slowly down the bar to her. He wore rimless glasses and a tie striped in maroon and yellow. He bent to her ear, touching her arm with soft fingers.

"How would you like to take twenty dollars for a good time?" he asked.

She could smell the whiskey and tobacco as she slid away from him. She ran to the door.

"Hey!" he shouted.

She wished Knockout were there in the Schenley lobby. K.O. would handle him. But it was her brothers all over tonight, suits, white shirts, and hands either calloused or soft.

Outside on the street she breathed deeply. In no one's face could she see that the man's rudeness inside the Hunt Room was carried with her into the gentle evening. Then it had never happened—the bad, and the good.

Donegan, it was a perfect moment. More than one opportunity. The time for subtlety was passing. She ached with the one last step to be taken before she became complete.

Then a letter came that read: "Friday night before the lions at the museum on Forbes. 8 o'clock. Please, please, please. But if you don't come I'll understand." It was signed, "A Gentleman."

Friday night she dressed herself in a bright dress with flowers. It had bare arms and a wide skirt. She put on pearls, a thin strand, and used a perfume she had bought especially for that night. Perhaps she would be mocked: there would be someone she did not expect. Or Donegan would change his mind, leaving her standing before the lions. It was an adventure and, she thought, she was beyond being hurt at expectations that failed. She would stand till eight-fifteen, then leave; and the evening would still be lush and filled with promise. She would twirl about in her dress with its large fanciful flowers. Her white summer shoes and her pearls would gleam.

"Hey, Princess," Bully called after her, standing in his stocking feet on the porch, "don't get run over. We ain't got no insurance on you."

She made her way down Robinson, past the statue of Jesus on the corner at St. Agnes—Bob Donegan had said he'd like to see it one day—and out Fifth. There was a huge crowd assembling for a baseball game at Forbes Field, but Fifth was still relatively free. People left stalled streetcars and walked briskly on foot toward the ballpark. On Forbes the crowd was seething. She hoped it wouldn't hold up A Gentleman: she would be on time. She saw the lions, and she crossed the street in the middle of the block before the vast lawns of the University of Pittsburgh to join the beasts in sphinxlike trances before the entrance to the museum. It was still as bright out as four in the afternoon.

She stood before the lions, and a young boy from Robinson, who lived four doors down the hill, came by. He wore horn-rimmed glasses and his name was Tim Mullaly. "Good evening, Maureen," he said, strolling past her.

"Good evening," she said, and watched him, a tall boy about fourteen. He was fair-skinned with ears that jutted out from the sides of his head. He wore a white, short-sleeved shirt in the heat, and as she watched, he turned about sixty feet away down Forbes and looked at her.

She did not know if it had been the boy who sent her the letters. It could not be. He was a dull boy; he stared at her only because it was unexpected that Maureen Scanlon, dressed to dance, would be standing out on the sidewalk thus exposed to the world. She ran across the street and boarded one of the stalled streetcars heading downtown back toward Robinson.

"We're not going anywhere, lady," the conductor said.

Maureen put in a token and said, "I'll wait."

She went to a rear seat and sat, staring straight ahead. He was not a boy who read, she thought, and he had no feelings. He was quiet; but it was silence that concealed stupidity. This wasn't a boy capable of writing such letters, maintaining a consistent flow, touching her with his gentleness and restraint. Turning to look out the window on her left, she saw Tim Mullaly standing there. He did not change his gaze. He stared through his large glasses at her. Maureen looked away. Somewhere she heard the clang of the trolley. Only she and an old lady bound for downtown were on it. After almost ten minutes of sitting, staring straight ahead, she could bear no more. Not looking to see if the boy still stood outside observing her—it was after all a coincidence that he had walked by the lions when he had—she rushed off the streetcar. The conductor said, as he opened the doors, "I never saw such a crowd."

The sky overhead had turned darker. There would be a night. But the clouds above still shone with the last of the July day. The crowds blocked Bellefield, the park out to Panther Hollow, down Forbes to Atwood and past: all seemingly men in straw hats or caps or bare-headed and sweating in the hot July night. It was the Philadelphia Phillies who called the horde out to Oakland, a titanic struggle in the night and fog lifting off the park. The warm, night air rang with the coming contest. The Forbes Field lights were already on. Men at carts sold hot dogs. Men carried infant sons on their shoulders. Bull-necked men in undershirts, handkerchiefs around their necks, put their shoulders down and pushed into the crowd. No one strolled. A fire lay at their heels as the men plunged toward Forbes Field, stepping on each other's shoes, elbowing, faces lit, Maureen thought, with some glory to be achieved down the next block. A streetcar's bell clanged and clanged. Maureen looked to her right and there rushed a phalanx of men who moved into her sightlessly, their eyes on the bright destination ahead. They spun her about. She stifled a scream. She did not want to be in the center of this charging herd. Ahead, she saw the flowing broad backs of men bent to go somewhere in noise and shouts. If she pushed, could there be an oasis on the sidewalk before the Schenley Hotel? She put down her head to rush there but was spun about. Seeing the library behind her now, she moved to push against the army in that direction and once more was turned. There were thousands of men, tens of thousands of men, hurrying to a place and to victories only they could recognize or understand. Standing utterly still under the soft, fleeing clouds over her head, she raised her face to the sky and tried to scream that she didn't want to be among men. Sounds died in her throat.

At the telephone in the drugstore next to the Schenley Hotel she dialed Donegan's number.

He answered.

"Bob Donegan, you bastard—" she began her condemnation, her words at last descending to earth like hawks free to ravage a queer, gray landscape.

THREE

Mortality

NEXT DOOR to the child prodigy, Alex Magruder, who played sad, longing melodies on the piano night and day, there lived on Dunseith a woman named Pauline Conlon with a good many hard years behind her. She was not yet fifty in 1938; still her years weighed on her face and in her eyes. They were years passed dipped in a brine of loss, doors closed, and abandonment. She had buried three husbands, respectively to tuberculosis, kidney failure, and heart seizure. Still handsome, whatever her years, it was remarked among people who knew her at the Irish Club that it was fortunate she had no children, given her luck, for what worse fate lay for a mother than to see a child depart before her? People died around her: the mother at birth, her father when she was a child, her two eldest sisters, and her three husbands.

Observing her from a distance and speaking casually to the thrice-widowed, early-orphaned woman, fellow parishioners at St. Agnes noted her charm and forbearance; but up close, hearing about her sisters, both of whom died of pneumonia in 1936 leaving families, and Mrs. Managhan next door on Dunseith, it soon became apparent that the woman, surrounded as she was by people meeting too soon their ultimate fate, Mrs. Pauline Conlon was not all—in a spiritual sense—she should be. The woman quibbled with fate, challenged religion by presumption, and was not a figure of heroic resignation and nobility learned at a dire price. She was, people close said, querulous and argumentative, small-minded: death tapping so often at her front door had taught her little. Was there nothing, a dread ran through her observers, to be learned from almost annual face-to-face confrontations with the last, melancholy reality? She acted as if she studied it, circled it, prodded it, and actually wanted to dance with death.

Her niece, a stout young woman named Mouse McHugh, came to put up her storm shutters in 1938, and she said the woman was impossible: a person would think it was her aunt Pauline who had suffered with pneumonia or lay at death's door in various deliriums, not the long parade of loved ones she had attended at their last rites. Mouse, like many people, couldn't wait to leave her presence alive. Pauline had, after all, that somber record behind her.

"I'm dying," she said to Mouse, in spring 1938, "of a disease nobody ever heard of."

"What are you saying?" the girl asked. "Human beings have been sick since the time of the caveman. As soon as they learned how to write, they began to put down their symptoms. Do you see those red leather books when you go to the doctor? They're filled with diseases; and one of them is yours."

"Medical science marches on, is that your meaning? You're not saying it stopped with the caveman?"

"I am not."

"Then every year—or ten years—the doctors discover a new disease. What I have is the disease they're going to discover ten years from now, in 1948, and a lot of good it will do me."

"You're not sick of anything, Aunt Pauline."

"Little you know. Put the windows up good, daughter. I won't be here in the spring when the new owner of this house comes to take them down."

When Mouse said good-bye, she also said, "I'll see you about."

Pauline pointed at the floor. "Six feet under is where you'll have to dig to see me."

Mouse left, confident Aunt Pauline was her usual self in mind and body. Sitting with Pauline Conlon at the Irish Club, people noted she nodded at each disaster and illness with grim recognition. "I have it," she'd whisper to Mrs. Magruder or Mrs. McCann, who attended the Irish Club with her on Saturday nights. She'd point to someone who had left for the restrooms. "That pain alongside her ear—I feel it at this minute. Lord, Minnie, if it strikes me at the top of the stairs, see that I'm lowered gently to the bottom. I don't want a battered corpse on top of the rest of what it'll do to me."

Taking a train ride up to Elyria, Ohio, to see another niece over Christmas, Pauline went to Father Farrell at St. Agnes. "Well, I've come to say good-bye," she said.

Father Farrell, then young and rather too pleased with his wit, which he had not yet heard repeated by himself over the next thirty years at St. Agnes, said, "It's very thoughtful of you, Pauline."

He knew full well what she meant.

"I mean until we meet in eternity," she said.

"Don't you worry," he said, "my health is excellent."

They sat in his office, a wintry sun falling between the blues and grays in the Virgin's gown in a stained glass window. The sun lit up Father's desk; it shone blue and gray from the window's reflection and the sun beyond.

"I'm not speaking of your health, Father," Pauline said. "I'm taking a perilous journey. Those steam engines go sixty miles an hour. I'm sure my fate lies in that devil's instrument." She stood. "And if you can't see the handwriting on the wall, then it's too bad that even the clergy these days don't take signs for what they are. I thought you'd understand: one of them engines of destruction goes to pieces every day, smashing into a cow or an automobile on the track, or just jumping the track altogether and leaving corpses strewn about in some poor farmer's field. Now, I never rode one before. They'll tell the story on me: 'Unfortunate woman took her first ride in an engine unsuitable to her fate and died forthwith.' A person hears that every day. First ride, honeymoon trips—people don't die on them things, Father, without a sign. I never rode on one, never intended to, and then Eileen insists, begs, cajoles, and here I go to my death. Father, I counted the trains in the paper leaping the tracks or banging into cows this week. There were two. Now, as a priest, are you going to tell me disasters don't strike in threes? Sitting before you is the third tragedy to strike this week about to happen."

When she stood to leave, Father Farrell said, "Stay a moment, Pauline." He took from inside his coat pocket a pen, and on a small piece of paper on his desk he wrote a brief note. He took a blank envelope from his desk, and said, "Before I seal this envelope with this note inside, I'd like you to see what I wrote." She put on her reading glasses and read: "Pauline Conlon will have no harm come to her on her train ride to Elyria, Ohio. I testify to the foregoing, Father Francis Farrell, December 8, 1938."

"Father," she said, "you can't say that."

"When you come back after the first of the year," he said, "you'll see I was a prophet."

"But I won't. I know I won't be back."

"Pauline," he said gently, "the odds are on my side. There's no reason to court death."

She later called him a presumptuous man. He could not know how the train was delayed coming back to Pittsburgh by a branch on the tracks; nor could he know the lurching and rumbling and death-defying angles on bridges, as they drove along the river, almost tipping in. She had barely escaped with her life. She smiled at Father Farrell in 1939 when she returned, but she never trusted him again.

Still a handsome woman, one night at the Irish Club, St. Patrick's Day in 1939, she was asked to dance by a bachelor named Duffy Kiernan. Mr. Kiernan lived two streets over on Darraugh in a house he had inherited from his family, alone, and in his fifties—in robust health, as far as Pauline could see—and he danced too closely. But she did not put him in place. He was a jolly fellow, clean-shaven, with short hair and a ready smile. They danced all night, and in the tumult of the place on the important night, Duffy whispered in her ear while they danced to "Stardust," "This is the best time I've ever had in my life." She touched his cheek and answered, "Go on."

They sat at a table with Mrs. Magruder, a woman named Breen who was visiting Mrs. Magruder, and a third widow, Mrs. Alice Long. And Duffy flirted with all of them, dancing with one, then another. Mrs. Long hitched up her skirts and stomped the wooden floor like a woman exorcising demons, and while Pauline felt she had an eye for Duffy, she was not worried. She knew men. Duffy Kiernan was hers.

Two weeks later, at supper in the Roosevelt Café on Center, he said, "I'm probably not much of a catch."

"Go on," Pauline said. "Women'd commit suicide to be sitting in this seat right now."

"You know what I'm going to ask."

"I do, but I'm not a mind reader."

"Then I'll say it: I'd be honored to make you my wife."

She took his hand—she had never done that before, acting the other times surprised and girlish—and said, "It's my honor, Duffy."

"That's yes."

"Yes."

Not a tall fellow, he stood and came around the table and kissed her on the cheek and squeezed her hand. "I ain't ever going to forget this minute."

Pauline held hands with him the rest of the night and they kissed hard at her door; but he did not come in. Both felt, hardly speaking of it, that now that they planned to marry it wouldn't do to have a single man and woman hanging about with each other in compromising situations. Pauline had held her other husbands to the same standard.

Her house having too many memories, Duffy and Pauline agreed to sell it, and she would move in with him down on Darraugh. While the old house on Dunseith was sturdy and Pauline would miss Mrs. Magruder next door and even Alex's piano playing, it wasn't as if she were moving to Ireland. She would be living two streets over, and she would not be leaving any of her old friends. She felt she had it all in her hip pocket once again. As flighty as when she had married Lawrence Plunkett at nineteen, she tasted youth once more. She had lived with Plunkett for eight years, and then Edward Boyle for five, and Peter Strong for fourteen. She had been a widow now for five years and thought Duffy Kiernan was the last: so rosy in his cheeks, his eyes sparkling like a baby's, and his skin hard and firm like a man accustomed to a great physical life. He worked as a timekeeper down at the Union Station. Every day after work at dusk, bachelor in habits, he briskly did five miles near-trotting out to Mellon Park in Point Breeze and back, a familiar figure rain or shine.

She did not know how to broach the subject, but he said to her one night, two months before they were to be married in September 1941: "I'm in as fine shape as that Tarzan swinging through the trees. The men in my family lose count of their years, there's so many of them. One of the grandfathers—it's in the church records in Mayo—lived to one hundred and ten. I hold no stock in bad luck, Pauline. In fact, as I figure it, the chances are with me, seeing the hard luck you've had."

They walked in the late September afternoon around the bowl of Pitt Stadium, and the air was turning cold with winter. "Duffy, it's my own well-being I'm thinking of," she said. "I have a quaking in my heart that sometimes starts to thump so bad I have to stop and listen to hear is it a radio playing somewhere in the house. In my face I get a sharp pain: it runs down my neck and into my shoulder. It worries me: I sit up in bed wondering if my turn has come."

"Dear woman," he said, "dear woman, let this old fellow take care of you. We'll live to see the Second Coming, I promise you."

In two weeks, on one of his daily walks, crossing Neville Street at Fifth, Duffy Kiernan keeled over, clutching at a telephone pole for stability but dead before his body landed flush on the sidewalk. Pauline, called by police, came to identify her fiancé at the Montefiore Hospital; and but for being grayish, he looked himself, and despite herself, she thought him a finer corpse than any of her three husbands. She was dry-eyed. She had not really thought he would not die. The night gathering, on the arm of Mrs. Magruder, she said, "Another one." And Mrs. Magruder said, "It ain't you, Pauline. It's the damndest thing, but it ain't you."

The fact was that no one at the Irish Club or St. Agnes condemned her either. If they were not already accusatory about her sorry list, one more person in her orbit passed away could hardly be grounds for asserting the poor woman carried about with her some quality that brought her relations to an early demise. After all, Duffy Kiernan and she had not been married. And engagement with a prospective groom dead on the sidewalk was—in a manner of speaking—a break with the long line of parents, sisters, and husbands who had gone to their rewards. He was not blood-related or legally bound, a virtual stranger, her friends said. Her niece, Mouse McHugh, however, stayed away from her, not answering her call in October to put up the wooden storm windows. "I have a terrible cold, Aunt Pauline," she said, wishing there were a central book somewhere where she could change the records, where it stated she was a niece and the other woman aunt, and simply scratch in "No Relation."

"You sound fine," Pauline said, "but I'm suffering, child. My head is as stuffed as if I inhaled a ball of cotton. I can hardly hear you, my hearing is that bad. Well, get better, Mouse."

At the bombing of Pearl Harbor in December, even Pauline forgot her recent sorrow. She read the news as 1941 ended, excited that the country had been attacked, attending Mass daily and the Irish Club on Saturday nights. It was a place to hear whose son had been drafted, who had enlisted, and then in 1942 who would not return. Buddy O'Rourke in a submarine; Johnny Quick in the Solomon Islands; Billy Keegan, one of two Keegan boys in the service, the other to return a morphine addict, in the perpetual mystery that surrounded reward and earthly punishment; and Pat Noonan, whom everyone swore couldn't have been older than fifteen when he enlisted, and sixteen when a sniper killed him in Manila. She rocked with their mothers at their wakes. She made fudge for the women, and but for the undue liberty in it, would have put up gold stars for each boy she knew who died in war, so keen was her sense of them as children, lads who had run barefoot down Dunseith.

As 1942 ended, she answered a knock on her door in a very cold December. The air itself seemed angry. The gray outside had almost turned to black, and only the tiny Christmas tree bulbs of yellow and red and green in the houses on the street lit up the darkness; and it was not night outside. It was noon, a damp, dark afternoon that might lend snow to the coming holiday, or might, Pauline thought, in a dour mood, stay black until the earth cracked open with desperation. She opened her door to the cold and stepped back at the sweep of air and the shock of the man on her porch. It was—in a sailor's suit, mackinaw up to his neck, body, flushed face, and baby's shining eyes—the late Duffy Kiernan.

"No," the man said, "it ain't him, I see by your face, it's his brother by one year younger, Sailor Kiernan, home for good."

She had heard of him. He had been in the peacetime navy and at Pearl Harbor. She had not known whether he was alive or dead: she certainly wasn't taking on the burden of the deaths at Pearl Harbor. Duffy had told her he had a brother and he was in the Philippines.

"I'll come in if you ask," Sailor said.

Pauline stepped aside and the man came in, making stomping motions and waving his arms, lively enough to shake her small Christmas tree—put up for the first time without her niece, Mouse, to help her, the child developing a rash of sore throats and fevers that would not go away. "Hate to bring the cold in," the man said, "because I'm all heat inside."

She had tea with him at her dining room table, Lawrence, Edward, and Peter mutely standing by in pictures on the buffet in great whirls of golden frame. "Poor Duffy," he said, "poor, poor Duffy. There's Kiernans still alive in Ireland who were a century old in 1900. I swear our people go to a hundred years of age and anything less is called unnatural among us. We had an aunt who was a hundred and twenty when a mule kicked her. And, dear lady, that mule was forty-seven years. It was something in the water, and we took it in our mother's milk. Poor Duffy is the exception that proves the rule: Methuselah was a Kiernan, there's no doubt."

"Have another cup of tea," Pauline said. "I'm not for gloom and despair and you're not a man who travels with them either, I see."

"Mrs. Conlon," Sailor said, "the morning of Pearl Harbor I was asleep on the USS *Arizona,* one of the finest battleships in our fleet, and I was more than asleep: I was dead drunk. But don't offer me a sherry, I haven't touched a drop of it since the Japanese bombed us that day. Not a drop. I know an omen when I see one. I wasn't even in the ship's crew. I was stationed in Honolulu and a buddy, a friend from some great days in ports in Africa and Australia, says, 'Sailor, come over to Pearl and you'll bunk with me and we'll talk over old times.' Well, I come over from Honolulu on a mail plane and we talked over old times Saturday night, swilling like pigs until dawn, and I came aboard the *Arizona* dead drunk, hardly able to walk, and fell into a bunk and slept like an angel—which up until that morning I wasn't. Then the Japanese come over in all their treachery and homicidal fury and put to rest our battleships and our fine boys serving on them. My friend, Gripps was his name, was one of the ones who went down with hundreds of others whose names are too sacred to be used in a casual conversation. And boilers were exploding and ammo was roaring sky high and the Japanese were tormenting us with shot and shell, and there I lay asleep, protected, Mrs. Conlon, safe as if I was in a cradle at my mother's bedside. They come to take ashore after a while the wounded from the water, and there I lay in a raft someone had put me into—I know who and so do you—and there was the dead and dying all about me and there was the mighty *Arizona* with all those saints on board settling into the ocean, a big coffin for youth, Mrs. Conlon, a big coffin."

Pauline bent over her tea.

"I was given a sign," Sailor said. "I never drank again and won't. I'm out now. I'm discharged. I got a burn on my leg in my drunken pig's stupor, and for that the U.S. Navy gave me an additional pension and sent me home. I was going to quit the service anyhow— too old, thirty years afloat, as they say—in two months and then the Japs came. Now I'll sell the family's house down on Darraugh and be off to a warmer climate. Except for present company, your Pittsburgh is a cold city, a cold, cold city, and I think maybe Jacksonville is where I'll settle."

In June 1945, Pauline and Sailor Kiernan were married. He sold the house on Darraugh and Sailor moved in with Pauline on Dunseith. He took to himself her attic, a warm room that rode atop the house like the highest reaches of a mast on a ship at sea. There he installed a telescope. Nightly, he went upstairs at eight o'clock to study the stars.

In unfailing good humor, Sailor helped Pauline keep the house in what he called shipshape. He vacuumed crevices she never thought of. He beat carpets. He fixed every squeak in every door inside and outside. He insisted on cooking, making only one condition, that the meals be exactly seven-thirty in the morning, eleven forty-five in the forenoon, and five sharp in the evening. He did the pots and pans and dishes after dinner and cleaned the table too, leading Pauline to the living room and handing her a magazine to read. He took her to the Irish Club on Saturday nights and drank Vernor's Ginger Ale while she and her friends drank beer. Sunday mornings he woke and attended early Mass with or without her. He was regular, healthy, talkative, and slept eight hours every night, going to bed at eleven and waking at seven in the morning like a clock going off. She heard him brushing his teeth exactly at 7:05 every morning. He would not hear of unhappy things; when she spoke of her ailments he put his hands to his ears. "It's a question of a smooth-running engine, Pauline," he said. "Long as things are shipshape, the longevity of the Kiernans is on us."

The man did push-ups every morning, a military count to his hundred and fifty. He ran in place as if devils chased him. When Pauline described the route Duffy had followed every evening as dusk fell, Sailor took it as a sensible course. He walked as his poor brother had every day out Fifth, making the fatal crossing at Neville as if it were his bathtub, on out to Mellon Park and back. There were no coincidences in the man's life, no omens about life or death, and, Pauline thought, not a scrap of sentiment either. If angels had gathered to whisper to him he'd live forever, he could not act with more confidence in his mortality. He was not the man to speak, even to his wife, if a holy conspiracy had been revealed to him about his good fortune and long life. She envied him at first, then began to mistrust him. All that lack of fear was troubling in a man. She loved her late husbands, who had been brave enough but not foolhardy where the last call was concerned. They had not quaked, but they hadn't coughed in the face of eternity ringing them up in her house on Dunseith. What would a man like Sailor think of death, he who had seen the best part of his nation's navy sunk all around him while he turned over in his sleep and blew drunken bubbles out of his stupor? The Japanese air force couldn't do it. What that walked, ran, or crawled on Dunseith could bring him to a reasonable fear of the unknown?

Sailor said her husbands' pictures on the mantel depressed him, and she put them away into a dresser drawer, but she could not feel at home in her own kitchen or any other room with a man like Sailor aboard. Watching him, she knew something otherworldly hovered about his good spirits.

"Tell me," she asked again, "when that battleship sank, there wasn't a sign you had at its sinking? Something you heard?"

"Only my snoring," he said, "if I heard anything at all. I was drunk as a log lying in the forest."

"The day before?" she asked.

"Nothing," he said, "I met poor Gripps and we commenced early and stayed at it late."

"You picked no special bed on the battleship?"

"No more than I chose what shoe to wear that morning. I did what I did. Sure enough, it was a sign to me: I never put one more drop of alcohol into my system."

She did not go to the Irish Club with him every Saturday any longer, affirming that it was not necessary for him to forsake his nightly telescope on her account. And after, she sneaked into her kitchen at six, after he had made dinner and she had claimed a headache to miss his five o'clock food, and ate by herself. She put a pillow on her ears in the morning when he brushed his teeth. Stretching in an exercise he did at ten minutes after eight every morning, he said to her—breaking off—"Pauline, you're not looking good."

"I feel fine," she said. "I am in the peak of condition, Mr. Sailor Kiernan. Don't diagnose me. There's Conlons lived until ninety. I don't have their birth certificates but my people aren't short-lived, you know. The tuberculosis that took my father killed seventy thousand people in the United States that year. We ain't a quick-dying breed."

"Why, I never said sick," he said. "I make no such implication."

"Well, a whole battleship went down," she said, "and the United States damned near lost a war and you walked away from the disaster with a scratch on your leggie. What else are you saying?"

She hid in her room the rest of the day. Looking at herself in the mirror in the bedroom over her vanity table, she noticed wrinkles she had never seen, small marks at the corners of her mouth that turned it down. The next week she had to have three back teeth pulled, and her face, it seemed to her, sagged away to old age.

"Do I look decrepit to you?" she asked Mrs. Magruder one night. "In God's name, don't josh me. I've been married two years now. Do I look twenty years older to you?"

They sat in Mrs. Magruder's kitchen, a sanctuary away from the tidy man with everything nailed down.

"It's the excitement of the marriage," Mrs. Magruder said. She was a woman of full width, large and hand-wiping with a broad apron she had been born in. Her own face was as unwrinkled as when Pauline had first met her forty years ago.

"But it's true," Pauline said. "I'm aging fast, I'm aging bad."

"I don't say that," Mrs. Magruder said thoughtfully. She went to her kitchen window and she looked out at a snowy yard.

"May, I've got to know," Pauline pleaded.

"Well, it happens," Mrs. Magruder said.

"He spies on neighbors with that telescope in our attic," Pauline whispered. "He cooks the food because he knows I can't bear it. He doesn't touch a drop, sitting back at the Irish Club and condemning us by silence. He makes mock of me by finding dirt in my house no human being could see. He wakes me every morning with that teeth brushing, scrubbing as if he had a stable he was cleaning instead of a mouth. May, I'm on the edge."

"Pauline," Mrs. Magruder said, alarmed, "you're in a state."

"Oh, that ain't it, May," Pauline said, taking good hearty Mrs. Magruder by the shoulders and falling on her in tears.

"How did I go on with all them already gathered in heaven?" Pauline asked. "I got ready every day. I said to them, 'Well, my beloveds, I'm not taking on airs about being better than you. I'm ready: no better than the ones I loved who went before.'

"But this one, this Mr. Sailor Kiernan: I abominate that man and everything shipshape so bad, damn him, I want to outlive him. You hear, I go about every day, saying 'Holy Mother, take him today and then me a half hour later. Don't let him see me go.' Him and his signs he pretends not to see: the man is going to outlive us all. We're just walking tombstones to him. It stayed away from me because I knew I was ready for it." She sighed and pulled away. "I'm a gone goose now and it's all his fault—I ain't ready anymore. I got the curse on myself now. I want to live too bad."

Sailor developed a cough. It turned to pneumonia. He was placed in an oxygen tent at the Montefiore and the doctors said his chances were fifty-fifty.

"Oh, my," Pauline said. "No better than that."

He beat the odds. He was on his feet in four days. He strode from the hospital as whole as the day he had caused the American fleet to fail at Pearl Harbor. In two weeks he commenced furiously brushing his teeth again and investigating Pauline's house for dirt.

On a cold winter day, shortly after Christmas, he insisted he would take a walk an hour before dawn. Temperatures were at five below in Pittsburgh. She knew—and she was right—he could not stay in the cold long. Not with weakened lungs.

The windows to the house had storm windows attached. He himself had closed over the storm windows wooden shutters to bar the cold. The house was wrapped as if microscopic germs might intrude from out-of-doors. No draft blew through the place. It sat weather-stripped, sealed, locked tightly, like something to be preserved from centuries of inclement weather for future generations.

He put on a mackinaw and said he thought the cold air might do him good, fresh off the night before the day's pollutions. The chill as he stepped out caused Pauline to fall back. Quickly, she barred the doors from inside. She put up all her night chains. She ran upstairs and put pillows on her ears. Even with the pillows she heard his pounding five minutes later at the front door. She heard him walk around to the back door. He pounded there, and then the sounds stopped.

In an hour she walked downstairs as softly as a stranger in her own house. Dawn was in the sky, gray and menacing in the cold. She put on a heavy coat and scarf to walk around the house outside, to find his body, to once more see death come to the neighborhood and not for her.

She found him sitting on the glider on the back porch. His face was as red as a tomato in season. His eyes seemed glassy with frost. "Are you there?" she asked, seeing he was not dead.

He opened his eyes wider. That awful sleep that had evaded doom at Pearl Harbor had fallen on him again.

The man had been comfortable as a baby napping in her glider in a below-zero temperature.

"I need some Ovaltine," he said. "My bones are frozen."

He sat in the kitchen in his stocking feet. He drank Ovaltine.

Pauline felt a terrible pressure in her chest.

"You're not ill?" she asked. "Warm enough?"

"Pauline, I worry about you. Why'd you lock all the doors? You're looking pale."

"My mind's going.

"I worry, sweetheart. I'm going to live a long time and I want my honey with me all the way."

"Oh, that's strange," May said later when Pauline told her. "A man in such fine health."

And she did not know Pauline had locked the monster out in the cold.

"We're crosses in a field to the demon," Pauline said. "It's a voice from the beyond calling to me."

Mrs. McGruder died two days after John Kennedy; and Pauline's niece, Mouse, was struck by an automobile in the parking lot of a restaurant on the Pennsylvania Turnpike, dying still clutching a bag with a club sandwich she was bringing back to her car.

Considerably older now than the people she saw on the street, Pauline Kiernan walked with less spring in her steps, but she was still able to go places on her own. Her husband, Sailor, was well known in Oakland for decades, briskly accomplishing the same daily walk for years—until he tripped over a cat on the corner of Forbes and Bellefield and was not able to walk as well after his broken ankle healed.

He and his wife sat on their porch in summer, smiling at neighbors, he thinking how life had been kind, she thinking things made no sense. Signs meant nothing at all or else they were inscrutable. Here the two of them were, old, getting feeble, and a person not able to tell what was coming to them or anyone else by word, deed, weather, or numbers, only that everyone died eventually, and what sense was there in that?

PART TWO

Special Types

FOUR

The Last Visit

I

AT THE high school where he had taught for thirty-five years and at the Irish Club where he had sat at more or less the same table for as many years, people who thought they knew him well considered the contentment that hung about Mr. Lanahan the result of finally marrying off his last daughter. Her name was Alice and she was an independent girl, choosing to live with her father after the other girls had moved out and her mother died. She and her father had taken lodgings at the Fairfax Apartments, and every morning he walked to his job at Schenley High School, where he taught art. If Alice was interested in men—she was thirty when the news was made public—she kept it a secret. She attended art shows with him at the Carnegie International, and when he had one of his own infrequent shows of his carvings, Alice acted as hostess, pouring champagne and greeting visitors to the modest gallery on Craig Street with enthusiasm, even passion.

At his art show at the Shadyside Art Gallery, where he assembled a lifetime of his polished and burnished wood carvings in 1962, she was everywhere, posing the *Press* photographers who came, trying to please the critics and the man in the rumpled suit from the *Pittsburgher* magazine. The night was not a success: another in a long string of quiet failures. No one had hated the complete retrospective, but everyone found that Jack Lanahan had ended where he started: his fantastical roosters—wings spread, claws thrust and beaks poised for love or combat, sleep or flight—hadn't deviated in intention or technique or themes one by one from the first rooster he had carved in 1939. He had carved hundreds, large and small, brilliant and sad, plumes erect and vanquished, but there had been no significant artistic progress, they found, no movement to indicate growth or promise, aesthetic consummations, or even that a self-conscious artist was at work. It was as if a man with some gifts toward expression had gone into a studio one morning and worked all day—and the day became three decades long—and in the evening when he left there stood hundreds of roosters all created under the same momentary impulse. Rooster drawings and statues became popular as designs, mass produced and everywhere, but not those Mr. Lanahan did.

Jack Lanahan agreed with the criticism but did not think it a bad thing. He had been under the spell of roosters from the moment he had started his life's work, and their general stale popularity, soon on dinner plates and doorknobs, had not diminished his own burning interest. He felt the same way about their vitality and ferocity, joy in existence, as he had when he first conceived of carving them four decades ago. At sixty-two, he knew roosters were passé: other people had appropriated them in tired formulas for napkins and alarm clocks. He continued to carve them as if he had discovered them that morning.

His stubbornness had tortured his late wife. Kate wanted first a recognition from him that an early marriage—he had been eighteen then, the young woman nineteen and a Presbyterian—had been a mistake. While his divorce a year and ten months later hadn't counted anymore than the marriage, a civil ceremony, Kate believed it was recorded somewhere in divine reckoning. Mr. Lanahan had had a child with the first wife, and Kate felt a soul had somehow been compromised and lost by her husband. The soul was doomed to wander eternity without hope of salvation. The baby was a boy and his name was Andrew, and Kate called him Andy and Little Andy as the missing child grew closer to her with the years. She knew each year what age his invisible presence had obtained. While Mr. Lanahan hardly remembered the mother's face and was undisturbed that the child was gone to his Presbyterian prospects and was not a daily reminder of the folly of a marriage that lasted less than two years, Kate saw the youthful error as the condemnation of a soul close to her. She wished Jack could see it: or at least suffer with her for the boy who would never know the God she, her husband, and daughters knew. On Sundays, she sometimes said, "I wonder where Andy is today." And when Jack didn't answer, she quickly added, "A lot you care."

It was this stubbornness in other areas too that came to lay a valley between them. She wanted some token also of his failure as an artist or provider to be stated, an acknowledgment that with all his bright early promise when they were married, his quiet wit, his care for her and the girls, he had not achieved anything. She wanted him to say, or if not stated that way, for him to change something about himself so she could know he understood he'd failed. He seemed to her pleased, even contented to be a high school teacher, never the artist who had hovered about the young man. She had thought him capable and self-sufficient. He had risen to captain in the army, but he came back to Pittsburgh never having left Arkansas, amused. She thought it abnormal. She considered him eventually spineless and lacking in daring. She told him so. Other times, she told him he was reckless with their futures, the lives of his daughters wasted by his daydreaming over roosters. She berated him for crimes he never dreamed of committing, and he did not argue with her. He had thought teaching public school honorable. He had admired his own teachers at Schenley High School. On Robinson Street, where he knew every son's plans as well as his own, he felt rather superior occasionally in his white shirt, tie, and suit every working day. After they were married, he had gone to Duquesne on the GI Bill. He had liked the respectability of it, his own father never pleased with his career as a maintenance man with the Hebrew Y on Bellefield, complaining of Jews and leaky plumbing and toilets that burst, things Jack never had to consider. That the times had turned his job into a refuge for middle-aged flops, he thought, was not of his choosing. But Kate saw it so, and he did not resist her contempt: it's not easy being married to someone like me, he thought, sorry he could not tell her or anyone his secret. It was simple enough. Jack Lanahan had "visits" as he called them to himself.

As failure dogged his path, a life perhaps in some lights not even having been worth living—no family of distinction, shabbiness, disorder, flight—and then the daughters, none marrying well, and the job, heartless teenagers who mocked his roosters and his studied manner of talking, and the neglect of his art, he discovered that he was a rare man, even a blessed man. He had visits from moments in his past, moments of such pure transformation that the ecstasy of their having happened stayed with him for years.

And they returned again and again. Unbidden, each transformed experience reoccurred, four in all, coming at unanticipated times and allowing him to relive them again before they vanished as abruptly as they had come. They were intoxicating and had been from when the first one came when he was in grade school, and Mr. Lanahan came to wait for them. He filled idle moments with the anticipation of their return. Sometimes years passed, but he waited. He came to remember in their full glory not only the moments that had seized him but each visit as the feeling of the experience returned.

Sitting in a first grade class, he again swam in an event that had occurred two years earlier. He sat there in wonder, letting the experience wash over him again, trying to hold on to it, but as quickly as it came, so quickly did it depart. He would have talked of it but he hadn't the words. Later, when he did know how to describe the sensation, he did not care to talk of it.

The event that set off the first visit had happened one day when he was perhaps three and it had snowed on Robinson, and he stood inside his home at the window hoping the snow would fall high as the housetops; but it stopped and the temperature became warm and the snow melted. His mother dressed him in a heavy scarf about his face and put on galoshes belonging to his older brother, and warmly wrapped, he was let outdoors. With him was another boy, whose name he did not know or remember, and the two of them fell into a marching rhythm in the snow, he and the other little boy sloshing in the soupy street, the tops of both of their galoshes flapping. A car coming down Robinson bore down on the other boy, horn blaring. The car skidded on the wet snow, turning and striking the other boy broadside, and the boy was thrown with a thump—not mangled or bloody, simply dead, both his galoshes thrown from his feet and the lad lying in the roadway curled as if he were asleep, shoeless, the galoshes too gone and the child dead in his stocking feet, asleep forever. Jack Lanahan suddenly felt one with the sound of galoshes slurping and stirring the wet snow: the skidding car, sight and sound together, then the bump and the boy in his gray socks alive, then dead. In the sight and sound, Jack was transported somewhere into the center of it, death at his own cold fingertips, his runny nose. He was for the moment the dead boy and still himself. Beyond telling, he was too the cold, metal car with its horn and the driver and the dirty sky over their heads. He had been filled with a transport of sudden joy that none of it was separate from anything else, only seemingly different until that second of apparent death— in a twinkling it was over and the happiness of his connection passed. Things fell back into place, and he screamed, "Mother, Mother!" and fell to sobbing by himself and would not be consoled.

Nights, a widower with his last daughter gone, he sat at the Irish Club, waiting, hunched over his beer. He had had some of the young men who came there in his classes at Schenley, and occasionally they came to sit with him. Other times men his own age he knew joined him. He did not take their heartiness as false or patronizing. Mostly none of the dreams that circled about the club had materialized for them anymore than their cigarette smoke, which hung on the air, ever became maidens in pale flesh and rosy tints or kings in raiment on camels and elephants. The smoke stayed smoke. His old friends were now as wrinkled as he was, had faced death and abandonment too. There was no one here to feel sorry for him; and he shared their lonesome journey, pleased they were there in the glow of the jukebox, mourning as each dropped away to death or success that took him to a better place to have a beer than the Ancient Order of Hibernians, Local No. 9.

But now, with Alice moved to Columbus, where her husband worked for American Airlines, he became a target for people wishing him well. He was regarded at the school as a man ripe for new friendships and at the Irish Club a prospective groom for Pal Mahoney's cousin, Maurya, who had recently come to Pittsburgh from London, and Paul Kerry's elderly sister, Ethel, who had been widowed twenty years. While Pal visited the Irish Club only on weekends, Paul Kerry was a bartender there and a constant threat: no sooner was Mr. Lanahan seated, neat of tie and suitcoat tailored to his spare frame, than Pete sent over a Heineken's and waved cheerfully when Jack looked up to thank him at the bar. Ethel was either in town for the week from her place over in Somerset—thirteen rooms and five baths—or she was staging a party for the Democratic candidate for district attorney, or simply anxious to meet Mr. Lanahan, whose artistic career she had followed with interest for years. Pal Mahoney's cousin was merely thrust at him on state occasions, and once, on St. Patrick's Day in 1963, he danced with her, a young woman so buck-toothed she hadn't a prayer, he thought, with anyone under sixty. He would have married again but for the recognition in himself of his folly the first times. Not that the blame lay anywhere but at his feet. He had loved Kate, and all that remained now of his lost love were two visits that came to him from her time like thieves in a doorway, leaping out and assaulting him with their memory of another time, one of the visits painful in its bliss, the other sublime in his love for the young Kate Carmody.

The great moment came when Kate, then nineteen, stood at a window on the third floor of her house on Zulema Street and called down in girlish jest, "Jack, I'm going to jump." He had looked up with a quick dizziness.

"Jump!" he shouted, in the grip of his sudden transport, truly hoping she would leap into the air and he would catch her. She had stepped onto the window ledge, and he felt no alarm that in her playfulness she would foolishly break the wood and inadvertently plunge down or simply fall. He knew he would catch her: the rapture in him soared until he felt he hovered with her at the window, even higher, and in his love for her, could prevent any harm that would ever come to her. He felt himself protected, knowing that in shielding her from hurt he would never himself be hurt with her. He saw no images of flight but only the two of them for one second free and unbound in unlimited space, neither air nor pavement, house nor separate person, and then it passed, and he shouted, "Stand back, Kate, you'll splatter the sidewalk," and she blew him a kiss and retreated from the window.

Now, in the procession of the thousands of memories that were embodied in his feelings about her, there was only the tangible visit of her at the window and one other to comfort him at their long love and marriage, which had gone sour for her but never—she would have called it due to his selfishness—for him. She had never disappointed him. He had expected worse. His family had died away before he was twenty. He had lived in their house with his mementos until Kate died and he had moved to the Fairfax. He had thought a man like himself who could not learn to be an artist, who had such strange impulses running in his blood, would surely never make a living and lie in a shelter like St. Vincent De Paul's in decline for decades and be an object of pity there among even outcasts. Still, his worthless job had seemed to Mr. Lanahan a continuous act of good fortune. He felt nothing for his students except for a favorite or two, the practice of education, his colleagues—with a few exceptions over the years—and gave no thought at all to his superiors, considering them inarticulate and shabby careerists who hadn't the wit to be humbled by their vulgarity and gracelessness. Among them too at school—the visits might come at any time—he waited for the calls from the sublime to visit him. He could not induce them, hard as he would try; they came seemingly of their own volition.

The last time he had been overtaken by an occasion that became a source of visits was when all the girls were small, twenty years ago, the eldest no more than eleven and Alice barely more than a baby. Dressed in their finest Sunday clothes, the girls and he and Kate had all gone to take pictures out at Schenley Park one Easter, and Kate had talked angrily on the telephone to one of her friends in the Women's Society at St. Agnes and called her friend back to apologize and then, Easter Sunday, had baked a cake to present her friend; and Jack knew it was himself that had set up the strange telephone call, the apology, and the white cake with chocolate icing that sat in the kitchen. She did not seem like his beautiful Kate in these moods but a pale stranger who had stumbled into his love affair with his wife. Standing before the flowers in Phipps Conservatory, she by turns remote, he lined up the girls in front of a tree at the entrance and then quickly turned playfully as if to snap Kate's picture in a gesture of goodwill. She said, "Don't you dare!" with a vehemence and a bitterness that shocked him. She knocked the camera from his hand and he saw it clatter to the hard ground, and the gesture sent him off into spirals of flight that would, he supposed, last a lifetime.

He had defeated her. It was in her anger as complete as death. In his losing at all of life's battles she considered important, but not conceding, he had given her nothing to hold on to. He had faded like weeds before the wind, not acknowledging loss. He had not grown ill and died young, like the men in her family, nor regretted daily a Presbyterian son doomed to hell; he hadn't lost his sorry job and they never knew want in their years of marriage. He had in his plodding way provided for her and the girls and carved his roosters. He was that day the same as the day he had started teaching art. He had forked no lightning. No one knew his name. She could not mourn him because he lived and wasn't sorry for himself; she could not even pity him because he wasn't unhappy. She could only feel that restless discomfort that had nowhere to light, and he embraced her anger in front of the Phipps Conservatory, knowing it came from extravagant love. Her distaste, he saw, held the two of them together now amid the smell of Easter and flowers in his mind, and he rocked with the two of them as if they were on a raft in the ocean. He was sorry he was such a disappointment, and he regretted she would never win. He would always lose, of course, not having her. Their eternal distance from each other, played out at the conservatory, made him giddy. It was real in a world of shadows. Then the feeling passed while the girls laughed and shrieked and Kate shouted, not unkindly, "Be still, won't you be still?" He had looked once more into a truth without words and felt marked by it. She would never know what he had seen: his greatest loss was their love. He had now only the memory of the conservatory and the girl at the window to bring Kate, whom he still loved, back to him. He had loved no one else and hadn't even the consolation of knowing he had made her remotely happy. She died expecting more from him than there was.

One day at his apartment house, he noticed a woman observing him on the elevator as he descended to work. He said, "Excuse me, I'm preoccupied lately. Do you nod at me and I ignore you? I don't mean to."

She said, "Yes, you do, but I don't think you're rude."

Outside on the pavement a light rain had fallen, and Mr. Lanahan squinted his eyes against the fresh June sunlight coloring the streets. The rain had stopped. He unfurled his umbrella. "I'm only here in the summer," the woman said. "I don't nod at you all year long."

"I thought not," he said. "I greet people in the fall and occasionally in the winter."

She said, "I have one of your carvings."

"Oh," he said, not knowing what to say. He seldom met anyone who was a stranger to him who had purchased one of the roosters. She said, "May I walk with you?" and he said, "I walk to school in this direction," and he pointed up toward Center. "It's a twenty-minute walk, and there aren't any buses that come back this way except by going across half the town," he said. "Why don't you walk with me ten minutes and then come back?"

She said, "Yes," but stayed with him until the entrance to Schenley High. It developed that she hadn't bought one of his roosters but, taking over a lease on an apartment from a certain Mr. Jacobson (who hadn't taste for anything, Mr. Lanahan thought, except his carving) had inherited the statue with sets of dishes and table linen.

He enjoyed listening to the woman, whose name was April Freiheit. She lived in New York and had come to Pittsburgh to be with her son and his children, but the children had grown and her son had left Pittsburgh and still she came summers, liking the city and the park, the museums, and the restaurants. "At this part," she said, pointing out to where Fifth was broad before the Cathedral of Learning and across it stood the classical columns of the Pittsburgh Athletic Association and the Syria Mosque, "Pittsburgh reminds me of Paris. Do you know, Theodore Dreiser said Pittsburgh was like Paris. Have you ever been there?"

"No," he said, "I haven't been anywhere. I always thought that if I traveled I'd be so preoccupied with my own thoughts that I'd never notice where I was anyhow. If it was London, I'd be thinking Pittsburgh things."

She said she understood, but she liked to travel because new places relieved her of her thoughts, and he accepted an invitation to dinner for that Friday night before she turned to leave. It was unspoken, he thought, that in one's sixties there was no point to cat and mouse. He had accepted dinner, no more. She had, he hoped, meant no more; and if she did she would be bothered by him—but he came Friday night, not wishing to annoy her. He brought a bottle of St. Emilion and she chilled it, and they drank it together after dinner. She was a widow with the one son, and she had enough money to come and go as she pleased. She had been to India and Japan, Greece, Morocco. She had lived in Spain. Jack's rooster, an elaborate flurry of blue and green feathers, sat in a corner, larger than Jack had remembered it. As they talked, he could see it. He wondered why he had carved it, why he had carved any of them. At eleven o'clock he thanked Mrs. Freiheit and walked down the corridor to his apartment. He considered the evening no great success, but, as he usually did before bed, he sat in the dark by his bed waiting to see if he would be visited by any of his events. They had not ever come as he waited for them as he prepared for sleep, but he wanted to give them one last opportunity before the day was finally over. He experienced no loss when they did not come. The visits gave him something to look forward to the next day. He had not had one now for four years, and it crossed his mind that perhaps it would never happen again, but he had thought that before, waiting as long as six years, and then the visit had returned in all its luminous glory. He went to sleep happily. Tomorrow he might again feel the power of those sacred events once more transporting him. In time, he accepted other invitations from Mrs. Freiheit. If she thought her first evening with him dull, she did not show it. They talked of her travels and his daughters. When the talk turned to art, Jack spoke as he did to his classes at Schenley, slow, measured, certain he was not making himself clear to her.

At his apartment at the Fairfax he had a small room, where he carved with a chisel his roosters and sandpapered them, then painted or lacquered them. He showed the room to Mrs. Freiheit one evening in July, as she gently touched the bird he was working on. "I would do something like this," she said. "You do this because there's enough novelty here to intrigue you, but you are not trying to attract attention to yourself. You just want to put something beautiful into the world, not yourself to be studied and made a fuss over. Am I correct?"

"I suppose so," Mr. Lanahan said. "Yes, I'm sure that's it. I really don't want to talk about myself as an artist. The birds are a way of working in art but of leaving myself alone. I don't know any other way."

He came to trust Mrs. Freiheit. They took summer walks into the park, and Jack told her his whole life had been spun out in less than two miles from where they strode on a footpath near the Westinghouse Memorial. He had lived with his wife and daughters in the house where he was born. He worked at a school a half hour away from where he was born. He could find within twenty minutes from where they walked fifteen men to hail whom he had known from childhood. His late wife had been born a mile away. "I know every tree in this park," he said with feeling. "My daughters climbed there, they ran on that hillside. I stood there and caught them as they ran and threw themselves into my arms. Once, there, Alice and Amy in a race rolled down the hill like barrels. Kate was furious. Their clothes were stained with grass." Mrs. Freiheit listened carefully. "Did you have a park where you took your son?" Jack asked her.

"No," she said. "Even when Harold lived we traveled. There were parks in various cities and countries, but we never took my son there. We just didn't, I wish we had. You've done so much in your life, Jack. You're in the middle of an adventure right now, being here in a place that surrounds you with things from your past, memories. Life is all one piece to you. For me, I'm still trying to assemble fragments. This country, that, this time; these people, I saw them once, I'll never see them again. Sometimes I feel lost, I'm sure you never feel lost."

"No, I don't," he said, and felt at last he had found someone he could tell about his great moments, slowly, describing each, then the visits. Mrs. Freiheit would understand. She was a woman who read a great deal. She would understand, but he hesitated. Would revealing his secret change it? Alter it to where he might never again experience one of his visits? He asked her to sit on a bench near the Westinghouse Memorial one day and took both her hands. "April," he said, "I'd like to tell you something about myself. It's very clear in my mind but I may not explain it exactly. I may lose it in the explanation, but I'll try my best. It's about my past."

"You mean your first marriage? When you were still a boy and your wife's unhappiness with the child? Are you struggling to forget?"

Mrs. Freiheit was a solid woman with features fine and sharply cut, like someone who had squarely dealt with the problems life offered: but now Mr. Lanahan hesitated. "It's all of one thing, my past," he said uncertainly. Did she wish to console him? He wanted none of that.

"We mustn't live in the past," she said, in words so often rendered each to each they had become the new litany of the despairing, turning their backs on the minutes and years of their lives, abject retreat from the responsibilities of having been there, suffered, gloried, praised days and nights or wept, as the case might have been. Not to embrace one's past, Mr. Lanahan thought, was to commit suicide retroactively. He had thought better of Mrs. Freiheit. Thinking she was making him comfortable, she filled him with dread at the promise of amputating him from times and places he loved. He did not mean to appear rude, but he stood. "It's too warm for heavy talk," he said.

Looking up earnestly, she said, "If it's too painful now we'll talk about it another time—but, Jack, you mustn't dwell on it if it hurts you. I'll share it with you. But take each day at a time. I don't dwell on things past."

The next day, thinking through the bright, early morning that he had escaped an awful misadventure, one that may have crippled forever things beautiful to him, he felt a pressure in his right side. He put down the chisel he carried and sat down. Perhaps he had strained a muscle in his side. It was not a place for the heart. He became bathed in sweat. Outside his window the street below on Fifth was quiet on a Sunday morning. The late bells hadn't sounded yet at St. Paul's Cathedral. The pressure in his side became a pain that tore into his midriff and into his neck and jaw. He thought it might be a heart attack after all and bitterly, with tears beyond the pain and the confusion that racked his body, thought his sudden death would mean there'd never be another visit. The last visit, four years ago, was it for eternity, and he so desperately had wanted in this dim present one more visit before he died.

I I

He woke to the sound of his name, "Jack, Jack, Jack," being uttered in a soft feminine voice. He said, "Yes," and started back to sleep, and the voice said, "Are you Jack? Do you hear me, Jack?" and he opened his eyes, and said, "Yes, I'm Jack." Two women, nurses, sat by his bed, and one spoke quietly, intently watching him. He asked, "Where am I?" His mouth was dry and it hurt. The woman said, "You've had your gall bladder removed, Jack," and he closed his eyes. He had thought her tone mocking when she said his name repeatedly, as if she spoke to a feeble-minded person, and as she was considerably younger than he was, despite the circumstances, he thought it impudent of her to call him by his first name. "Mr. Lanahan," he said softly, and closed his eyes against her.

Alice came from Columbus, where she lived, and May. He sat up in bed to greet them happily, as always, seeing the children there when he studied them rather than the young women. Cathleen, Amy, and Elizabeth sent flowers, and Mr. Lanahan felt at peace with himself. In the long hospital hours he could think over the remarkable moments he had once lived. He knew each second of the experiences, but the magical feeling of them still did not come. He lay in bed reading, receiving his visitors, bored with two of his colleagues from the school. Pleased and alert when Matt Breen and Ned Durgan came with Oscar Lyons, he sat up happily. They grouped themselves around his bed like physicians in medical consultation, men his age who had known him each year he and they had lived together since birth in Oakland. He studied their faces, wishing he could tell them how he differed from them but wanted to share the treasure of his secret blessing. But Oscar was bent on Mr. Lanahan's soul and there would be no telling anyhow.

"I don't like it, Jack," Oscar said. "You could have gone to your death in an unhealthy spiritual condition." He had a successful garage and Gulf service station on the boulevard, and his hands, gnarled and blackened at the nails with oil and grease, could fix a ruined car with two paper clips and a pack of chewing gum. He too was a widower and had learned his trade with the marines at Tinian, Saipan, and Iwo Jima in World War II. Now he was grizzled, never quite shaved, nothing of the gallant boy about him; and Jack closed his eyes momentarily against the sight. He saw again Oscar Lyons with forearms burly as Popeye's, profane, brave, and unconcerned about his soul whose peril lay decades away in a distant future. "Oscar, I never harmed anyone," Jack said. "It'll go good with me." And he thought, only Kate. And God will understand that; it was one of His insoluble situations He presents us with.

Ned Durgan, who was known as "the president" because of all the company of boys at the Irish Club he could once seduce women the quickest and in the greatest numbers, said, "It's not a joking matter, Jack. You don't go to church often enough and you don't take things seriously enough. Artists always have this tendency toward atheism."

Mr. Lanahan closed his eyes again to recapture Ned the boy, but the lad with curly black locks wouldn't come, only the wrinkled fellow before him, bald and rather heavy lipped. "I'm as firm a believer as you, Ned," Jack said.

"No consolation at all," Matt Breen said. "Let Jack be: I sense martyrdom in the room. He's testing God. He's twisting and turning little tricks on our Lord to see what he can bend the rules to. Educated fellows always try this path; I've known dozens up to the same game."

"Thank you, Matt," Jack said. "I really do court martyrdom."

Oscar brought up Tim Phelan's recent death, and that started the friends talking about Ryan, who had died young, and Peter Veilely—who had, to everyone's amazement as they counted the years, been dead forty years now—and the late Roscoe Grimm, and Chesty Mullins, and poor Biff Chambers, who could have outrun and outplunged Franco Harris and Rocky Bleier together on an ordinary day except that he had never fully recovered from pneumonia after high school and died early. "He could run through a brick wall," Matt Breen said.

"And Cleet Cavanaugh!" Ned said. "Set a car at sixty miles an hour coming at him and I'd pick Cleet's noggin to come off winners. And jump. I remember observing the fellow five feet over my head one Thanksgiving in an Oakland Community–Irish Club game."

"I see Cleet now and then," Oscar said. "He's not doing well. Heavy and drinks too much. Another one of your intellectuals who's got a rabbit in the hat he's going to play on the Holy Trinity."

Their talk soothed Mr. Lanahan, the clear sentiments of love and embrace, ultimate justice, worth, the natural universe an orderly place to be observed in all its levers and gears and wheels from accustomed seats at the Ancient Order of Hibernians, Local No. 9. Jack slept when they left, feeling things were in place.

Two days later, Mrs. Freiheit came with Alice, and his room began to crackle with change and purpose. He looked over their shoulders out to the sky over the parking lot at the Montefiore Hospital. He would have flown into the far sky if he could have. In the face of their excitement and expectations there was no escape. They cast off between them the old Jack Lanahan and laid before his eyes a new creation, vibrant, wanted, and successful.

They had sent slides of his roosters to New York, and two galleries had called back frantically. He was, at sixty-three, to be launched. He lay in the hospital room tense, hoping he would fail. To have denied the women their game of making him famous would have been too direct a role for Mr. Lanahan. Always he could count on nothing happening to him, aside from the rich storehouse of memory he had accumulated for himself; he did not expect much would come of Alice's and Mrs. Freiheit's meddling into what he considered his slow, honorable decline. Instead of a graceful slide into oblivion, he would not—except for the full, rich moments of ecstasy lost to him in another visit—have cared if the stabbing pain he had recently suffered were part of his last second on earth. Death, he thought, under terms when he was not called on to collaborate with a noisy world was preferable to his present state: waiting to see what would happen to him in New York. It distracted him from his preoccupations.

Alice and Mrs. Freiheit duly crated and shipped up to New York more than forty of the roosters, some done twenty-five years ago, some lately, that he had kept in an old warehouse down in Soho owned by a cousin of Matt Breen's. Even in that neighborhood, where the cobblestones in the street were scarcely safe from theft, they had been safe for decades. He waited with dread, teaching school on his recovery from his surgery as if lead were his father in tones more suited to a funeral oration than to fifteen-year-old sculptors, whom he bored even beyond the usual. He refused to go up to New York for the show and knew the tide was running against him when the turnout was big at the opening and the sales were large and he began to get letters and long-distance phone calls. Alice stayed in Pittsburgh to attend to his prospering affairs, moving into her old room at the Fairfax. She said her husband bored her. Mr. Lanahan feared she had found a new career for herself.

In the first two months of his new fame, he sold thirty-five thousand dollars' worth of his carvings. He idly wondered whether he should wreck the rest down in Soho: take Ned and Oscar and perhaps Billy Carroll, who had once fought Chesty Mullins to a two-hour draw over whether Davey O'Brien was the greatest small quarterback of all time, and with crowbars and hammers smash this unpleasant future which beckoned. He did not answer the telephone. When other teachers at Schenley came up to congratulate him in the smoky faculty lounge—a story ran in the *Post Gazette*, after the one in the *New York Times*—he nodded curtly, smiled, and walked away. He had always been known as someone vaguely eccentric; now, he hoped no one would take it personally.

He began to avoid Mrs. Freiheit and Alice. He took long walks by himself, pleading a slow recovery. In the fall the trees in Schenley Park grew stark and brown, the branches traceries against the pale sky. He touched the wood, removing his gloves. It spoke to him of living things he would like to carve there, shape, put the spirit of the wood into them so that bird and living wood would resonate together, and he sighed with the futility of it. Someone would comment on it, buy it, admire it, even cherish it, but treat it like a possession, not something that was supposed to have a momentary hour and then return to the earth to become further fulfilled in corn or wheat. He would have liked, he thought, to be one of those cunning men who strung together old toilet seats and random wiring and hubcaps and called the accumulation of a lifetime "The Celestial City." No one ever knew what to do with the collection of rambling garbage can lids and broken toasters and let it sit for years, shiny and queer, until the wind scattered the pile of trash back to its natural elements. Listening to how well he was doing from the two women who dogged his steps nightly at the Fairfax, Mr. Lanahan was vexed and unhappy. He felt it was Kate's vengeance; she had punished him from Heaven for his composure at failure and his Presbyterian son, disrupting him with the thing he dreaded most, acceptance. He fretted, trying to find a solution for himself, waiting for a visit, but it was a lost, nervous business. He could not concentrate. He was subverted daily by news of his success.

I I I

"Alice," he asked one day as the snow lay deep outside on Fifth, "was I a good father?"

"Yes," she said. "When we were children, the other girls and I were proud of you. We'd bring other kids to your studio to see your carvings. We were the pride of the neighborhood. At school, people knew you as 'Mr. Lanahan,' and we were 'Mr. Lanahan's daughters,' as special as if we were the children of movie stars. And at home, alone with us, you read to us and interrupted your work on your birds always—to talk to us, to chase us around the rooms with an old broom. We haven't been completely happy, any of us, in our marriages, I suppose, because none of our husbands measures up to you."

"Fancy that," he said, watching the snow pile up against the window. "But I never made your mother happy. My work distressed her."

"Oh, you're wrong: she loved your work. She brought the ladies from St. Agnes in to see it when you weren't home, not letting them touch anything—swearing them to hold their hands in their pockets—and she stood back proudly and watched their faces. Her face glowed when she said, 'Don't disturb your father down there,' to us. Her heart went into every bird, each wood shaving."

Mr. Lanahan said, "I never saw it."

"It was," Alice said, "the way the world up till now reacted to your art that inflamed her. She loved you and wanted to protect you from other people's meanness. Every show you did was a trial to her: the people who didn't appreciate you were all her sworn enemies."

"The numbers were legion," Mr. Lanahan said.

"It was all personal to her," Alice said. "Your work was you and she loved you."

Mr. Lanahan stared into the falling snow outside the windows, its dancing configurations and depths. "It must have been my first marriage then," he said.

"She never spoke of it to any of us," Alice said.

"It tormented her, the fate of my unbaptized son."

"It bothers me too," Alice said.

"Who is to say, if we had raised the boy a Catholic, he wouldn't have been a bad Catholic and suffered a terrible fate?" Mr. Lanahan asked. "I'm not a very good Catholic myself; and I don't suppose a son of mine would have turned out better."

At the Irish Club that weekend he brooded at a table, and when Billy Carroll passed, Jack called to him. "Billy," he said, "I was thinking of you this week, your fight with Chesty Mullins. Join me for a beer."

"Well, one," Billy said. He went to his table and came back with a bottle. He was now in his mid-sixties, and still men spoke of his famous fight. He and Mullins had been friends before it and never spoke a word afterward, one or the other rising to leave when his former friend entered a room. "It was a right that ended it," Billy said, stepping back before he sat and striking a fighting stance, and

Jimmy Ahern, walking by on his way to the men's room at that moment, said in passing, "I saw it all; Chesty beat you by a mile." Billy whirled in quick rage, but seeing old Jimmy Ahern said, "Oh, it's you, I thought I had another enemy to drop." They squeezed each other's biceps, and Billy sat. "It was the fight of the century," Billy said. "Chesty started it by saying no Irishman had the brains to be a quarterback." The men had started the fight in front of the White Castle on Forbes and battled several blocks away into the park over a two-hour period.

"Billy, do you dwell much on the past?" Mr. Lanahan asked.

"Me, no. I live for the day."

Billy Carroll's children were in another city; his wife was dead for thirty years. He had really only that memorable fight to hold on to, all else about him seemingly vanished.

"I live in the past a lot," Mr. Lanahan said.

"I know you do," Billy said. "I see it in your eyes."

"Billy, I think I'm going to be a rich man, maybe famous. I'm going to be a late arrival at sixty-three."

"Well, better late," Billy said, drinking his beer from the bottle. "If you don't mind my asking, Jack, what is it you do when I see you here at the club, sitting here quietly over the decades, sipping beer for four hours and lost to your thoughts? I'm not a detective, you understand. But I've watched you, lad. What are you thinking?"

"Of nothing in particular. I'm waiting."

"Waiting!" Billy said. "I won't ask for what?"

Billy had once been a barber, another time worked on a circulation truck for the *Pittsburgh Press*. He had driven a bus for the Transit Authority. He had come to his sixties by a hundred jobs. He and Jack Lanahan had sat next to each other at St. Agnes's in the first grade. He turned now to stare at Jack, directly into his face, close enough that Mr. Lanahan could smell his heavy breath and note each pore in his wrecked old nose.

"Am I an odd duck?" Jack Lanahan asked. "You're studying me."

"Yes, you are," Billy said, starting to rise. "But the world fell apart a long time ago, Jack, for me, for everybody. Better times took a walk. So what the hell! You're in one piece, better than a fellow could say for the rest of the world." They shook hands as elaborately as if one were leaving on an ocean voyage and the other would stay on the pier. Billy tottered across the dance floor, skirting dancers and tables. Alone again, Mr. Lanahan thought of the first memorable visit he had experienced when he was a child, not yet able to talk. He wished, in the confusion of his new triumph—unwanted and untasted—he would have a visit from that time, to feel once more the rightness of himself.

Almost from birth, it seemed, he had been frightened of a hallrack in his room on Robinson, with its arms and metal grasps where people hung their hats. Its shadow fell on the wall, and he was too young to explain the thing had arms and a mouth and could walk as the shadows wavered on the wall behind it. He screamed himself awake at night and pointed at it. He was no more than two and regarded as nervous. When he pointed at the hallrack, no one knew what he meant, but eventually, when they did, they moved it out of his room. He dreamed it stalked him up the stairs from the first floor, and he saw it nightly in its accustomed place near his bed. But his father, who was not home much—he supposed it was women; his father seldom drank or gambled—caught on to his terror, and he brought the hallrack up to the room where the boy lay cowering from his fear of it and dismantled it, tearing off each limb and leg.

Watching, Jack had gone into a paroxysm of delight, wild and limitless pleasure that there was no hurt anywhere, or future pain, or seemingly hard things that weren't transitory and couldn't be broken apart, dismembered and rendered safe. It was all somehow pieces of wood and no danger. He had felt himself part of his father's hands, capable of seizing threat and fragmenting it, and, blissfully, he had felt himself move into the empty space where the hallrack had been, the wall bare of shadows now, into a place of absence of evil or danger or grasping or clawing, mutilation or pain. In that place of absence he had felt free and boneless and knew it was where angels dwelt, light and floating, airbound and boundless. He was at one with things that lay behind hard things seemingly permanent and all that people ordinarily sense. It had been only a reeling moment; then he drifted down to an ordinary comfort that his old enemy was in pieces, and he kissed his mother and father and slept soundly.

Standing uncertainly in the Irish Club, he thought he would not have a visit from that moment tonight. He was slightly drunk, and the visits seldom honored such occasions. Old inconsequential Bing Crosby sang on the jukebox as he left. Jack wished as he made his way down the long stairs to Oakland Avenue, then up Fifth to home in the new winter wind, his father would come tonight and tear up the victory that now lay on him and with it its shadows on the wall, dismantle it to pieces, so the boy could sleep like angels in a place absent of harm.

FIVE

A Mystery

H E WAS known to all who drank and traded in truth at the Ancient Order of Hibernians, Local No. 9, in 1944 as Jaecko Doherty. He was the son of one of the venerable doormen—who afterward never permitted his name to be mentioned in his presence. But in his time, as the newspapers developed the story, in the years before the television cameras could bring a scholarly public sights of the very houses, the women, the restaurants, and the beaches where he had performed his wonders, he had many other names under his ample belt. He was known as Lester V. Flegal of Tucson, Arizona; Joseph Horvath of La Mirada, California; Lawrence K. Pfeister of Willock, Pennsylvania; Harry Oleander of Jamestown, New York; and Peter Paul Ryan of Centipede, Wyoming; and once, to a woman he had known for only two hours before he married her, Calvin Coolidge of Washington, D.C.

Unremarkable physically, he was remembered as being rather on the shortish side, an inch or two under the five-foot mark, and not slender as a gazelle. He had, in fact, even in the poor newspaper photography of the period, a belly that jutted forward like a torpedo in search of a destroyer to sink. He wore thick glasses, and when he was absorbed in his thoughts, so the story goes, his glance wandered about in his head, unfocused, seeking with his eyes the ceiling or the floor, far corners in broad, disconnected sweeps. He had small, delicate hands like those of a fat child. To disguise his soft, fall-away chin, he wore a beard, which had turned prematurely white. It lay in no particular shape on his chest, neither Santa Claus luxuriant nor trimmed precisely to indicate a practical mind. To men, of course, he would have seemed unappetizing: to women, one would have had to ask them, and the mystery was why none of them would answer.

The usual fanfare accompanied the man's story once it was revealed: he had married sixty-two—or was it thirty-eight, or ninety—women, and none wanted to press charges against him even though he had taken money from them. Two in 1944 had gone to the police in Flagstaff and Seattle and complained that their husband had vanished, they feared foul play; and they wanted Missing Persons to find him. Whimsical, he had described himself to his many brides as a secret agent for the Spanish government, or an American spy, a nephew of Adolf Hitler in hiding, a defrocked priest, a gunman from Mexico sought by friends of the late Leon Trotsky. The women who went to the police thought it was Hitler or perhaps the communists who had done him in. He was secretive but stoical about his make-believe lives. The women said he laughed about his varied enemies: he made them laugh too, or cry. He was quite the most admirable fellow some of them had met, and they married him. As the story broke and more women came forth, it became apparent Lester K. Flegal, or whoever he was in his heart, was an extraordinary man. The numbers of women he had married—absconding with an automobile, some jewelry, cash on hand, nothing spectacular, no closed-out bank accounts or ruin visited on his wives—became legion, as part of the mystery, the numbers, and then the love they still bore him. How had he inspired it?

The ramifications of Jaecko's elusive charm had a deep and wide effect among the men in Oakland who pondered it. No one could detail these adventures in Jaecko's wake for certain, since historians of the period from Oakland were generally in the armed services and the youths patrolling the streets had no great regard for tradition. The older men at the Hibernians still held America itself and its peculiarities as an aberration in their Irish pasts. They always knew a villager in the old country who had somehow done less or more. But it was a fact, two weeks after Jaecko's mystery began to unfold, his cousin, Marty, left his wife.

Marty Doherty, about thirty-two at the time, two years older than Jaecko, had been married for fourteen years. At eighteen he had married his high school sweetheart—rather, the girl he had loved when he dropped out of high school at sixteen. He and Eileen had four children, and Marty abandoned in a flash all five of them. The news spread quickly; and it wasn't long before Marty Doherty was discussed as frequently as his more famous cousin. Lacking the white beard, Marty was in his way as uncompromisingly ungainly as Jaecko. He too was shortish, perhaps an inch taller than the notorious Lothario, and he too wore thick glasses, but he did not peer about in abstracted visions like Jaecko. He was not quite as plump as his cousin: his abdomen was as ripe as a small watermelon but not as imposing as the menace of an advancing torpedo. It was conjectured that Marty had taken Jaecko's homeliness into profound consideration and said quite simply to himself, "I'm not half as ugly or graceless as Jaecko, and I'm willing to settle for half of what he did," and left home that afternoon. Perhaps he thought, "Twenty women will do me; I don't need eighty."

He was gone three months in 1944, the day's news swallowing up even Jaecko. The Allies were advancing in both theaters of war, and even the very young boys, twelve and thirteen, followed the maps in the paper carefully for news of brothers and cousins—and their own fate at the draft board.

Marty had never been a regular at the Irish Club, and he was not missed.

He was arrested in August down in Beckley, West Virginia, about five hours out of Pittsburgh, for bigamy. He was living under the name Harry McCoy. He had been seen by Eileen's uncle, a Pennsylvania State Highway patrolman, who had gone into a diner for a hamburger and there discovered the runaway bigamist working at the grill. He wept—some said with pleasure—when he was returned to Pittsburgh in manacles. He had married one woman only, a widow named Spriggs who owned the diner and was apparently looking for help when her late husband, a short-order cook, had died. "He seemed fishy to me from the start," she was quoted in the *Post Gazette,* "but there's a war on, you know, and I took what I can get."

Returning, Marty was put on probation after the woman in West Virginia—she was twenty-two years older than Marty—divorced him. He came back to Oakland and his children, was seen pushing them merrily in strollers around Schenley Park, trundling them on his shoulders, and holding hands in the Strand Theater with Eileen, his wife of many devoted years. It was assumed he felt he had had his chance and found the game was not genetic. Pal Mahoney, a casual friend, affirmed that Marty Doherty swore he hadn't been influenced in the least by his notorious cousin. But there were many skeptics at the time.

"It's the sex," Cleet Cavanaugh said, speaking of Jaecko in the May the war ended in Europe. "The man has some technique. He knows how to do something to them; he gets their bodies on his side and then the mind follows."

Cleet had missed the war because of his shoulder. He trusted that the truth of things lay in physical processes. Johnny Bain, who was at the table that night at the Irish Club in 1945—and suffered from a club foot—might generally have agreed with the older Cleet. But it was too simple. Johnny was sixteen: he sought complicated answers. He moved his hands about as if he were wrapping a package.

"You see," Johnny said, "he gives them what they want but it's not a sexual thing. He plays out for them what they expect from a perfect mate. He puts himself together like a tailor-made suit. He reads them like a fortune teller. The stories he tells—and they're good ones—are what wraps them up. He's a chameleon. Where most fellows miss out is they don't know what a woman wants to hear: about herself, or the situation, or the man she's with. That's where the fellow is a genius. He looks into a crystal ball, you see, and he says, 'Lady, you're going to meet a tall, dark stranger'—or whatever it is. He might say, 'You're going to find your little dog and I know where to look.'" Johnny searched for the words. "He gives them hope is what he does," he finally said.

Young Bain's analysis was not greeted with enthusiasm. He had stolen Pal Mahoney's very argument, and Pal was six years older. No one at the table liked Bain's effrontery; he was too reasonable for that hour of the night. It was late, but if dawn was in the third-floor windows of the Irish Club, it was disguised by the pulsating red clouds outside. The mills still roared with steel for the war in the Pacific, and even the darkest night held uncanny lights. "Wait a minute," Pal said after thought. "It's a matter of numbers, son. The fellow flips enough switches, I say he's going to get motors going somewhere. I say if the man's record is sixty women, he tried his devilish wares on one thousand sixty of them. Go out-of-doors—it's a fine night—and talk to enough souls even at this hour and you'll sell a gross of shoelaces. The trick is not in the laces or some quality of yourself. The trick is in the numbers. You may have to talk to three thousand people, but one hundred and forty-four of them before daylight will be walking in shoes held together by your laces, if you have the stamina for it. I give the rascal credit for persistence. I'll award him even a high mark for keeping his nose to the grindstone. But I'll be damned if I honor him with ability there, or charm, or talent. It's numbers."

Pal Mahoney always took the side of the family as an institution in any discussion. He saw in vagrant Jaecko as real a threat to the old values as if the man were all the defense plants in Pittsburgh that had taken women out of the home and put them behind a lathe or set them to wrapping parachutes.

"I knew Jaecko when he was a kid," Corny Sullivan said, now an authority who was unchallenged. "One day Sister Agnes sitting there at the piano in the fourth grade, banging away, and shouting at us to sing, says, 'If there's anybody here too sick to sing, I'd like them to come up here.' And there's Jaecko to the front of the room—as healthy as a cow a minute earlier—staggering, holding his forehead, reeling up to Sister like a dying man. I never saw the like: the boy put on sickness like a glove. He was pale, he was sweating, his knees were giving out under him. He was a pitiable sight. Sister stopped the music right there. She thought she had a dying youth on her hands and was set to prepare the boy for last rites. Why did he do it? For amusement: Jaecko loved playing parts. Anything you'd suggest to him—being sick, an automobile going up a hill, a cloud—the fellow could do it. Now what if Sister Agnes, gone before some of you were born, was of a marrying capability instead of a nurse and nun at heart? Why, she'd have married the fellow to participate in his game. Do you all see my point?"

As Corny was the oldest person at the table, everyone nodded. "But," Kiley Dodd said, "I could ask the next ten women I meet up here at the club to dance with me, no matter how I asked, and I'd get ten turndowns, twenty if I asked twenty of them."

Kiley, who became a sort of bank robber after the war, took it for granted his listeners understood he meant the paradox in his extraordinary good looks and Jaecko's ill-favored bearing. When Kiley got out of jail in the early sixties, foolishly having been enticed to drive a getaway car whose motor wouldn't turn over at a crucial moment, he heard again and again he resembled Elvis Presley. He hadn't heard of the singer at Leavenworth, where he had been serving three years, and was puzzled.

Yawning, Pal said, "This absorption with a scoundrel bores my ass. I'm going home. Virtue may be dull, lads, but it'll stick to your ribs after the cream whip ain't remembered."

He was correct, as it turned out, at least in Jaecko's case. After the initial newspaper accounts, he was not mentioned anywhere except at the Irish Club, where his memory was occasionally honored among the mysteries of the place. No law enforcement brought him to account for criminal conduct, and he never came back to Oakland. One risked his life to ask his father about him.

As five o'clock arrives, the men at the table in the Irish Club stand; someone stretches wide. Sunday morning in all its dignity and promise is acknowledged to be on them, and each greets it in his fashion.

Cleet Cavanaugh thinks as he lurches home, between the expectations of football triumphs and the sick aunt, who had come to tend his younger sisters and who now needs attention herself, that if he knew Jaecko Doherty's secret, he would not stoop to pilfering their purses but would choose women so adorable no men could conceive of them and go from one to another until he died in exhaustion. Amos Kelly, who had been sitting quietly at the table, too old to look forward to a life much different from the way it is now, thinks that Jaecko Doherty must have known something. He thinks if he had known what Jaecko knew, he would have moved away from his old, domineering father, with whom he still lives at fifty. Corny Sullivan broods about it before sleep and decides that it is all an exaggeration of the newspapers: there were no more than two women, perhaps three. No man as dumpy as Jaecko Doherty could have been the source for such miracles.

The night is particularly dark, but the steel mills from the South Side light up the clouds with their red fires. The sky itself seems to be a red, churning lake above Pittsburgh. The redness of the clouds touches the sides of buildings and lights up windowsills, red bars, red stripes, the streets white but glowing. Johnny Bain thinks that it is only because he is sixteen and has a bad leg that he has up to now been denied information that Jaecko had. When he is older and walks in places where his brains are praised and admired and his leg forgotten, he too will sweep women of all shapes and sizes before him with a power he can almost taste in his mouth. He will know what to say and do when the time comes. All of them, all who have ever heard of the mystery of Jaecko Doherty—the contemptible, fat midget who cared for not another soul in the world—are shadowed by his squat, bearded, thick-lensed legend. He falls behind them as they make their way up Robinson and down Forbes and through life, sometimes forgotten. At other times he prances on ahead of them, beckoning with one pudgy finger for them to follow him.

PART THREE

Local Irregularities

SIX

A Girl like Sheila

B Y THE time Jimmy McKenna had returned to Oakland from Korea, his mother told me, he was pretty much a lost cause. He did not want to attend Duquesne College and take sound pharmacy or accounting courses but said he had decided he wanted to be an architect and attend classes at Carnegie Tech. She'd stop me on Robinson Street in the glow of a late Saturday afternoon as I made my way down to Oakland and the evening's promise and say, "You there, Clifton, do you drive your mother to an early grave by unnatural connections among people who would shock her if she could hear the atheism that's their common tongue?" I said I did not, and while Pitt was somewhat suspect to Mrs. McKenna, it was not like Carnegie Tech, where there may not ever have been a Catholic play put on and no holy picture ever painted and no priests or nuns about to give the place solemnity, balance, and a student and his mother the sense that even undertakings as solid as architecture were not frivolous. "He came back from war with his values more ruined than his poor body," she told me, leaning on her porch railing, seeing me frequently at the Irish Club on Saturday nights with Jimmy and other boys. "Have a word with him, please. There are courses at Pitt he could take—he didn't have to plunge all the way down. I envy your mother: she gets two good nights' sleep running."

Both of Jimmy's elder brothers had gone to Duquesne and hadn't regretted it, and it seemed Jimmy had gone off in his own direction, if not downhill, to the local critics on Robinson and at the Irish Club. He hung about with young men with horn-rimmed glasses in the farther bars on Forbes, out near Tech, and occasionally walked about with an older woman, head bent and not looking up when friends passed. When he came to the Irish Club on Friday nights, he brought a book—not an unusual circumstance—but he drew lines on a napkin with a dark pen and put the napkins away in a shirt pocket.

One night he announced to us at the Irish Club that we didn't think large enough. "Do you think skyscrapers get built by men whose minds are set to putting up shacks? I developed some perspective, seeing something of the world." The fortunate among us lived in single family houses on Robinson or Dunseith or else Forbes: the rest, like me, lived in the apartment government complex called Terrace Village II. "We might as well be in a hillside village in Korea," Jimmy said, "for all the big things we think. We're down because we think small."

We saw Sheila that night for the first time. She wasn't unattractive but not to Mrs. McKenna's taste. "I don't like that blond dye," she said, "I think it makes a thin woman like that one look consumptive; you know how pale a tubercular gets in bad light. But she does have James Donald by a few years, so I suppose there can't be anything serious on either of their minds."

Sheila was Irish and Catholic and lived with her widowed father in the Fairfax Apartments. They worshiped at the great cathedral on Fifth, St. Paul's, rather than the more modest St. Agnes at the corner of Robinson and Fifth, bordering the Soho district and Oakland. Soho itself was still the home of an occasional respectable family, but below it immediately was the wild mix of nationalities and colors at the Brady Street Bridge, and while Mrs. McKenna would make no apologies to anyone for the parish at St. Agnes, she knew others, like the finely dressed and coiffed Catholics strolling to the cathedral from their expensive apartments at the Fairfax, might consider these people of a lesser social status. She wanted no one to think that a son of Irwin "Red" McKenna, a city fireman for thirty-two years until he died of influenza, wasn't as good as any woman he would choose for a wife. I heard her say, "There's no one in our family who has nails that length. We have no need for unnatural adornments." From the Fairfax Apartments, every morning, rain or shine, Pie Traynor, the legendary Pirate third baseman, walked downtown four miles. But Mrs. McKenna did not consider herself second to anyone, or her children or her late husband. Neither, she said, did she aspire to put herself above ordinary people by living in expensive apartments on Fifth near the Syria Mosque and the Pittsburgh Athletic Association and taking Mass at the cathedral. The Bishop lived on the cathedral grounds: Mrs. McKenna said she did not have to live with bishops.

There was something, as it turned out, dark and disturbing on Jimmy McKenna's mind about Sheila, if not sinister, as Mrs. McKenna understood the usual complex of emotions between men and women. Jimmy was rather shorter than the average and not at all heroic in shoulders, arms, or hips but flat and square and pale and with blue eyes that were uninterested but followed everything, as if he had no control of his natural curiosity.

He was rejected as a suitor by Sheila for probably sound reasons, and then Mrs. McKenna had to face another prospect: Jimmy dropped out of school altogether, even a place that might coddle offenses against the natural design of the universe. Jimmy sat about staring into his beer and talking all night long about battles in Korea, and one day went down to where Sheila worked in the office of Gimbel's Department Store and tried to present his case to her. He had heard that the young woman had taken up with someone at Tech and apparently planned to marry him.

Sheila accompanied Jimmy downstairs to have coffee with him

in the store's first-floor restaurant and thought the matter had been resolved there, she later said at Jimmy's trial, when Jimmy began to smash up the adding machines in her office to make his point and rip pictures from the wall and fling them across the room and throw wastebaskets through the second-floor windows. The security guards were called and later the Pittsburgh police, and Jimmy was taken for mental evaluation down to Western Psychiatric Hospital.

His stay there went past a month, and after a time it was obvious more than an evaluation was afoot. Jimmy was sent out to Mayview, where long-term patients resided. Jimmy was being treated, concern shown for him, because of his good war record. And when he was released, he seemed quite fine. He was pale and assured and talked with knowledge about the Pirates' statistics. I saw him that Friday morning, and we had two hamburgers each at the White Castle on Forbes and made plans for a pitcher or two Saturday night at the Irish Club. But that afternoon after he left me he went directly downtown to where Sheila worked and, after about five minutes of trying to persuade her to have a cup of coffee with him downstairs, began to smash typewriters with staplers and then throw the staplers at the vases in the room and kick apart the furniture.

This time he was confined for more than six months at Mayview. On a cold day at the end of the winter, I drove out to the institution with Corny Sullivan, who was a second cousin, in Corny's new Buick, a Regal in black and gold he had bought used for a song.

Jimmy seemed quite himself. "She loves me, you know," he said, sitting on the edge of his bed in a dressing gown. "If ever I can get her out from that fellow's influence, she'd see. You know things passed between us that seldom transpire between a man and a woman. It is physically impossible for that woman to love anyone else, take my word for it. Things were said, things were done—and she knows it. She could no more love anyone else than she could marry a St. Bernard. I'm everything to her but she won't face it. I get angry with her sometimes about it, but then I forgive her. It's her, you see, that's the way she is: and I love her for it. She's like a child that has to learn with time."

"You're not going down to that department store again, are you?" Corn asked. He played the trumpet and wrote music too. He planned to go to New York when his father's health improved.

"Corny, I'm not mad," Jimmy said, "I sat through mortar fire in a ditch with water thirty inches high. I know reality as well as the psychiatrists. The department store has seen the last of me."

We all shook hands warmly and planned to have a beer soon under the Miller sign at the corner window at the Irish Club.

I did not see Jimmy when he came home. He hid from us, but his mother said he was doing quite well. He took a job on the South Side at Jones and Laughlin and avoided us in Oakland, and I graduated Pitt and did the best I could. It was in the newspaper that I read, after a few years, that Jimmy had accosted Sheila again, now married, at a bus stop, and when a bus driver and some of the passengers on a North Side bus had intervened as Jimmy tried to argue his case to Sheila, Jimmy had pushed the driver and caused a passenger to fall to the pavement. He was, this time, sent to the institution for three years, and none of us visited him. When he was mentioned, hardly anyone spoke of his unfortunate passion, but he was remembered for something at the Oakland Community–Irish Club football game on Thanksgiving or a memorable baseball game at Forbes Field, where Jimmy had worked with us for years selling hot dogs and popcorn and pennants.

His mother, one night in 1964, told me he had been released from the institution and had enlisted with the U.S. Army to serve in Vietnam. "I pray for him ten times a week," she said, "and a thousand times in my heart. I never thought he would go again to war, but he loves his country, and if we do not win there the communists might be anywhere next. Have you served, Clifton?"

"Yes, I have," I said, "but never in warfare."

"There are things only warfare is stronger than," she said. "You know that."

On holidays sometimes Mrs. McKenna lifted her skirt to her knees and danced to Irish songs and sat back at her table and clapped her hands to the trio there for the occasion. Her face shone, and she said on St. Patrick's Day and Christmas and sometimes on a Saturday, face shining: "I've never had such a time as I've had tonight." Both of Jimmy's older brothers had ended their marriages in divorce without children, a turn to affairs that Mrs. McKenna, who had a complexion like light dancing in the liquid in her glass, said had deadened her soul to life. But, she said, she still had high anticipations for Jimmy, who, after all, hadn't married and could make her a grandmother yet.

He soon came home, wounded and dazed, leaning on a cane, gray, wrinkled, his eyes old, the boy reciting his lines from plays gone from his voice and pale blue eyes. He limped into the Irish Club and was greeted by old hands, some of whom hadn't heard from him in a decade. For hours he showed us helicopter maneuvers with his hands cutting the air, and with his cane pushed back the Viet Cong and dug into earth burrows to liberate mountains. "Boys," he said, as dawn came, "I missed you all. I thought of you often. I saw your faces in the night when I stared into the darkness."

On Monday morning, two days after he had arrived in Pittsburgh, he took a taxi out to where Sheila lived with her husband and children in Monroeville, in the suburbs, and when Sheila called the police, Jimmy was arrested and sent away for an indeterminate length to Mayview. He fought the police and threw a rock through her window, but he was not charged with any crime.

I saw his mother some months later at the Irish Club, and she asked me if I saw Cleet or Pal Mahoney anymore, and I said, "No, they go their ways and I go mine."

"Some of the faces here," she said, "are familiar; I've seen them for years. And some are strange to me and don't even look like people used to look. But I hope you don't ever forget your old friends."

"I think of Jimmy often," I said, remembering the pale boy who had become memorable in my mind for an inexplicable obsession. He had, probably, not spoken to Sheila more than four times in his life.

"I go to visit him," Mrs. McKenna said. "He's in the Veteran's Hospital at Aspinwall, now." Her face was shrouded in secrets, memory, and loss. She sat with an old maiden aunt named Estelle, who daintily put away a pitcher and a quarter on Saturday night and had her hair done twice a week. "War is terrible," I said.

Mrs. McKenna laughed and took the sleeve of my coat. "Clifton," she said, "I knew your late mother. She died proudly, I'm sure. You're a good boy. You used to walk by our house every day, so I talk to you now like someone who's still a little older and wiser than you. I'm as cut off from future life as Estelle here, no grandchildren, as if my late husband and I hadn't ever walked on the earth. There'll be none of us soon, and what are we being punished for? There's little worse that communists can do to a man and his mother that a girl like Sheila—for all the handshaking with a bishop—can't do better."

SEVEN

The Payment

LONG Conall O'Brien came home from Vietnam without any apparent disabilities. He had been there for two years, and what
was wrong with the known universe wasn't in his large frame or
brain but in the atmosphere in the United States. By 1973, he decided, the time of whores was done, women generally being more
accessible to sexual congress than they had been when he was a boy,
and hence there being levied on his expectations a sad end to a
comforting circumstance Conall had regarded as eternal.

"Whores," he explained to Pal Mahoney, a friend from the closed
Ancient Order of Hibernians, a week after the airplane had arrived
on American shores from Saigon, "are as old as the Bible. King David,
Solomon, your best people, lords and monarchs participated in the
ancient practice. I never held myself better than the old Hebrews. I
admit to you the institution fell off in high spirits with the coming
of St. Paul, a man ready to cast the first stone at the prospect of an
honest woman turning a coin with what resources were open to
her. Up there in Belgium I know they taught you that."

Pal Mahoney had gone as far as Louvain decades earlier in his
pursuit of a vocation with the Jesuits, and when he had not re-
minded someone of his credentials for serious metaphysical discourse,
the other person brought up the subject. "I think you miss the point,
Conall," Pal said. "It wasn't a question of honest labor involved—it

was more purity on St. Paul's mind. He was thinking of the human race generally, the protection of the young, the consolations of the family, the dignity of women in a society where a Roman lout was liable to knock off a hand at the wrist to a woman that crossed him. The point was prostitution was dragging down the human race, not elevating the sorry creature who did her all for a roof over her head or a fire in the hearth."

"Harmless," Long Conall said. "To love a woman and change your mind and walk away after she does what she can is unclean to my way of thinking. Let women stay pure without my two cents' worth: I for one never intend to use them, deceive them, tell them lies as if I were selling a carpet sweeper, and do my ho-ho-ho better-luck-next-time as I retreat down the stairs. Give me a prostitute, no hard feelings either way. I'm not hurting someone's sister or daughter; I'm not damaging a sweet young woman with a picture of herself in a confirmation dress on the mantel. Love is love, sex is sex, and never the twain shall meet."

"And marriage?" Pal asked.

"Not for me," Long Conall said. "But I'm not a freak; I have my needs."

The abnormal desire for bought women, he thought, might have been the shame of another man's life. What golf on Sundays was to some fellows, visiting the girls was to Long O'Brien. A man with a photo hobby downstairs in the cellar under the steps—a darkroom with chemical mixes and his own enlarger and pictures hanging by neat clothes pins—Long O'Brien would never be, not with the golf game, the photo lab, bird-watching, stamp collecting, and reading of history, poetry, or theology all wrapped into that one sinful habit and good time, recreation and philosophy. He lived for being with the whores. In Saigon he had known Asian women; in San Francisco, some as white as the sun on morning dew; in Pittsburgh, black girls with a lamp's light playing on their brown arms and thighs and in their dark eyes. When he wasn't with them, they sat about in his imagination, in robes of flimsiest fabric, the garments falling open on couches and carpets where no one knew shame, lounged on beds, propped up by an elbow and smiling their exotic smiles at him.

Extraordinarily tall, by a whisper able to enlist in the Marine Corps, nearer to six-foot-nine than anything, when Long O'Brien walked among prostitutes he felt arrived and at home. When they giggled and said, "Hey, skyscraper, come down here," he laughed with them as he never did when strangers mentioned his height to him. "I make you my size," an Indonesian girl had said to him, and Long let her, giving her another twenty for the good feeling she left with him. Under the streetlights, beneath the bridge to Homestead where the cobblestoned streets with the whores were, he strode about nightly as a young man, never more at ease and contentment. He breathed in the night air in Homestead from the age of fourteen on, not particularly tall there, although he knew for a fact he was, not called on to be brave because of his size, or good, or to stand out. "Your head bumps the clouds," a girl in front of one of the houses said to him when he was sixteen, and she was right, he thought. People expected great things of him; but he knew early it wasn't there. He was no leader, no debater, no scholar, no warrior, and not even ambitious to succeed in ordinary things. And among whores, they understood: in their calling he was always, bless them, another john, no more, no less. They always told him he was just fine with them in sex, made simple jokes with him about his considerable size, and stayed in his memory with the power that religious services had for some men, their children growing up, holidays, and women they loved.

He had lived with his mother in a house on Ward Street, a block from the Metropole, where he stopped for a beer every night on his return from the whores, and his mother died while he was in Southeast Asia. He had been stationed in Da Nang, driving officers in staff cars for a year, then working in personnel at headquarters in

Saigon; and when he came back to America, his mother had died, the house on Ward was empty, and the whores over the bridge in Homestead were gone, victims of the changing morality. There were still whorehouses on the North Side and in what was left of the Hill District, a number of apartments with free lancers out in East Liberty, but the noisy streets with hustling girls upstairs and cardplayers downstairs in Homestead, fellows from all over Pittsburgh laughing and joking among themselves on the sidewalks, were over. They were such summer nights he knew would last forever in memory. Waking in the middle of the night in Vietnam, he had lulled himself back to sleep with daydreams of the lounging girls in his mind, sweet and gentle, adoring, seldom a wrong word, precious at ten times the price. On his return to Pittsburgh, his visits to the old places, trips to new brothels, were marked for him by a stirring of old excitements and remembered promises. He could hardly feel where he was or see the women who lay naked next to him for the other women, years and years of them, who came back to breathe on him, whisper, delight him with their acceptance and joy in Long Conall, one of them. "Pal," he asked, "do you ever feel the old times so bad it crowds out what's before your eyes at the moment?"

Pal Mahoney was hovering about his middle forties and had never been married, his only brides first the church, which he had embraced as a boy going almost to the altar to become a priest, and then the marriage to the company of his boyhood companions, savored over almost twenty-five years at the Irish Club. He had seen young men take their first beer and later become alcoholics, and he had seen young fighters named Irish Tim or Terrible Billy Hogan with knockout records of 19 and 0 become wasted stumblebums cadging a drink: families separated, women deserted, men grown sick and never returned to the Irish Club, an old world gone, a new one nowhere in sight. He was there like the fans, the disinfectant in the air with the malt and yeast, the dancers' feet on the wooden floors, the jukebox with songs fifteen years behind the times. "Do you mean the war?" Pal asked.

"No, damn the war!" Conall said. "I wasn't thinking of it while it was happening and I'm not thinking of it now."

"Your mother and father?"

Good Pal Mahoney, skin shining fair and unmarked with his normal understandings of decent people: Conall could not tell him he himself was haunted by scenes of whores maybe long dead, pale white women who came and went like snowmen in their own time, not to be honored except in the heart and memory of a sport of nature. In his loneliness, Conall decided that he was being given signs he had become too old, twenty-eight, to hang on to childish things and the time had come to fill his empty house on Ward with a wife and children, commence the times appropriate to a man trying to fit in to society. He held a good job; it was not even to become wealthy, but with a wife throwing in her oar, the house paid for, the sum he had saved from Asia, he could make a fine new life. Before the war he had worked at the Carnegie Museum in Oakland, wearing a blue serge guard's uniform and a stiff cap, looking a proper representative for culture, and they gave him back his job when he returned. He had enjoyed being among the statues and paintings and thought he would die on the marble steps among the columns— if not in the arms of a young woman calling herself Margo or Roxy— but now he thought he'd listen more carefully to job possibilities in the air. Kevin Costigan had told him he'd be a natural in personnel work and to come downtown and see him at his office, and Conall thought he would one day soon.

It seemed foolish at first, fastening on a young woman like Irene Ahern, but he knew her brothers and was well-thought-of among all there, and when he joined them regularly at their table at the University Grill no one thought it strange. He had been friends with them since Central Catholic, and when they invited him for

Easter dinner in 1975, he asked, "It's not too great a strain on your mother?" and was assured it would not be. And Irene up close was as beautiful as he had remembered. He had seen her at a distance in the two years since he'd been home but wasn't sure she'd recognize him. She was several years younger than Conall, and even ten years ago there might have been the question of why a young woman twenty-three years or so of age wasn't married; but today she and her friends, about the same age, came and went in their tight-fitting dungarees and no one raised an eyebrow. He had watched her grow but had never been to the Ahern house. The table was spread with ham in pineapple sauce and sauerkraut on the side. The elder Aherns had been married for more than forty years, and lifting a glass to toast the happy occasion, Conall found himself tenderhearted and warm as he said, "To the happiest family I know." He had determined to marry Irene Ahern, and later she admitted that she had entertained the same thoughts about him. After dinner, she walked with him to his car, a '72 Nova known, he thought, before every bordello left in Pittsburgh and not ever seating an Irene Ahern in it. "I stop for a beer down at the Metropole some evenings after work," Conall said, inhaling the soft fragrance of her hair, as he opened his car door. "Do you ever get down there?" She said yes, she knew the place, and if it was an invitation she'd look in on the next Wednesday.

"It is," he said, "it's an invitation. And thank your mother for the food. I'm not going to eat for another week."

Or, he thought, driving away, seeing her trim figure in his rearview mirror recede, sleep for three nights waiting for Wednesday.

They were married seven months later by Father Farrell in St. Agnes's, and Neil Ahern, Irene's eldest brother, was the best man. Pal Mahoney was there and attended the reception at the Aherns' home; and with him Tom Shannon, who had lost a leg in Vietnam; and Brian Smith, who had become a drunkard after Korea and never wrote a line of poetry on his return; and Kevin Costigan, an old neighbor, and his brother, Bob-bob; and Tail Burke; and Ryan Carmody, a once-famous skater with the Ice Capades, and his cousin, Matt Breen, who lived in Las Vegas. There were girl cousins and aunts dancing about, and Conall, towering over everyone, had his tuxedo shirt smeared with lipstick. When he caught Irene's eye she winked and he winked back. They had not lain together in the long months before their marriage. They had embraced and kissed the whole night long on her downstairs sofa, but when the moment became feverish, Conall stood and left. He had not taken her to his house after dark. It was a new life he wanted. Irene was a beginning. Never again, he thought, would he revert to his old ways: children, Easter dinner, a new car every year, brothers-in-law to catch a football with in Schenley Oval. He would find love with his wife. Leaving, Pal Mahoney hugged him, and said, "You're a man, Long Conall."

Conall and his new wife drove that night in his new Buick down the Pennsylvania Turnpike to Washington, D.C., where they stayed at the old Mayflower Hotel for two nights, drove down to Mount Vernon, and strolled around the grounds, holding hands like high school kids. Conall thought he had missed much in life, smiling at strangers, and with Irene he was going to recapture it all. In bed with her, at first he was awkward and subdued, but he told himself, she is a woman after all, and handled her as if she were one of the summertime girls he had known from Pittsburgh to Saigon, and then it went well. His boldness swept her up. His sureness made of their nights and beds comfortable and accomplished arenas of closeness and certain truths, and, he thought, finally love. "There's something I must tell you," she said, as they lay one morning in the quiet of a Maryland motel en route home. He turned and touched her lips with his finger. "There's nothing necessary," Conall said, thinking, I'm no angel.

Back in Pittsburgh, with one more day of holiday left, he called Kevin Costigan for an appointment to look into the matter of becoming a magnate in Personnel Recruiting. He sat contentedly on his small back porch looking out at the porch of the house behind him. His mother and father would rest easy now for their tall son. Irene had walked up to Robinson to greet her parents, and Conall had stayed behind to vacuum the house, and when, after a long hour watching twilight set on his yard, he came back into the house he became aware a crowd had gathered there, silent and lost to themselves.

Women from his imagination sat about in his living room with his mother's old tasseled lamps, throwing their shadows on his mother's carpet, leaning somnolently on the arms of couches where he and his family had sat for a generation. Conall rubbed his eyes, at first amused. When he opened his eyes again the silent Asians were still there, the fantastical blond woman from San Francisco, and with her a dark-haired beauty from Da Nang with her straight coarse hair down to her waist. Naked, some observing him, others in clothes of silk and half-slips, they sat waiting for him to make a decision about them. Conall knew a hallucination. He went back out-of-doors, quietly closing the wooden screen door.

He sat on the back porch again, watching night fall on the bushes and the roofs of the houses next door. The apparitions would be gone when he returned, he thought, and tried to see in his mind the configuration of light and shadow inside that had caused him to believe the whores who had constituted the only joys of his life had reappeared to haunt him. He stood after twenty minutes and went inside. They were still there. He turned on the lamps and the whores still sat about as surely as if Mrs. Sally O'Brien's parlor were their natural home. Conall walked out the front door to the sidewalk, feeling faint, and waited for Irene. When she came, he swept her up and carried her upstairs. Lying with her naked on his old bed, among his Marine Corps tunics and polished shoes, pictures of his high school class and mother and father, he kissed her neck and her shoulders, not daring to turn to confront the women from his imagination who had assembled in his room now, leaning in doorways, smiling gently with promise at him.

"Is there something wrong?" Irene asked two days later. "No," Conall said, "it's just going back to work again. It's a jar after our days together." At the Carnegie Museum he did not see the women of his youth again, except in his mind; it was only in his own house they apparently chose to gather, to mock him in his marriage. He tried to conjure them up at the museum, but they would not come. They appeared only at their own whim in the house on Ward.

After a month of it, concentrating in his own home only on Irene's dear face or the television set, he decided to speak to someone about it. But Pal Mahoney, he thought, would cite him just such a case that had driven a monk in a Swiss monastery mad in A.D. 916; and Father Farrell, looking into Conall's face, would say, "Serves you right, Conall. Did you think you could break all the rules without paying a price?" A psychiatrist would be the man to confront with it, but it was not the ghostly women who now teased and tempted him and horrified him in turn he could not talk about. No, the problem was elsewhere. It was that he clung to the darling creatures of his past: he did not want to risk relinquishing the sweet joys of remembering them as they lay in his mind. He wanted them to leave his house. He did not dare losing them as they resided on waves of goodness in his mind.

After another month, Irene said one morning, "It's me, isn't it? I've done something wrong. Or you've heard something. Tell me, Conall, is it something I can explain? I offered to tell you everything the first weekend we were married." She put a cup of coffee before him where he sat at the kitchen table. Her face was wet with tears. He stood and bent down over her and kissed her. "Never cry for me," he said, trying not to see the two women who stood at the screen door to the yard, one smiling, the other running a comb through her long hair, the light from the morning sun racing the length of her bare arm down her silken leg to her thin ankles. He held Irene closer, then harder. "Never mourn me," he said.

Two weeks later, Irene left. When he came home she was gone and her clothes, the alarm clock she had cherished since grade school, the picture of her brothers, another of her mother, one of her father in a World War II sailor's uniform. Her hairbrushes were gone from the dresser. She might never have invaded Sally O'Brien's house, and Conall walked from room to room, observing that where there should have been an emptiness with her absence instead now lay a rightness of things as they once were. He supposed the long lost women would retreat now, go to the grottoes and caves where they had come from in his mind. He looked about and could not catch them full view. As he looked, they dodged: one moment there, another somewhere else. But there were fewer of them. He smiled at what he thought was a remembered young black woman from a sacred day when he was seventeen and he had reached quietly to touch her as she took off her robe and she had pressed his hand to her body as if to say, "Don't be tentative with me, Long Conall, we're friends." She was gone, however, in the twinkling of an eye.

He watched television that night alone and later strolled over to the Metropole. A Pirates game from San Diego was on, and Conall sat with Ryan Sheehy's younger brother, who sold used cars. Conall stayed through the entire game, a tight contest. He went to bed at midnight and thought if he saw any of Irene's three brothers in Oakland he would speak only if they did first. He wondered if Irene would divorce him. He would not call her to ask her to return. As far as love went, he supposed he had known it with her, maybe not, but he did not want her back. He was not, it appeared, a man for catching football in the street with his son. He went to work the next day, jaunty in his uniform, chatty with a group of schoolchildren touring the art gallery, flirting with an elderly librarian he brought a Diet Pepsi from lunch. After work he went home, showered, changed from his uniform to a short-sleeved shirt, and drove his new Buick to a place he knew on the North Side on the other side of the Allegheny Center Apartments. He was cheerful as he was admitted, stood quietly while a girl jumped to show she could leap as high as Long Conall stood.

"Here," he said, taking off his shoes. "That'll make it easier."

He resumed his popularity among the whores, as if he had never left. He savored the feel of the old times in his return.

The tall fellow came to visit like a monk regular at Vespers, and would, he thought, until the powers that had given him breath took it away or caused his unnatural passion for whores to dwindle and dim. Undoubtedly even certain stars and planets in the solar system in time waned in their shining and explosions.

It was no surprise, though, when one late afternoon in September, arriving in boyish anticipation, he saw at the head of the steps—over the swaying buttocks and dyed blond hair of the prostitute he followed—his recent wife. Irene stood there in the whorehouse looking down sadly at the spectacle of Conall and the woman ascending to her. She did not change expression.

Long Conall looked away, but he knew she would be there when he glanced back, probably there every time the foolish man went on about his pastimes. She would be somewhere, in a room, on the stairs, at the door, sitting on the edge of the bed, if he knew his luck.

She did not intrude in the pleasure of his time with the whore.

Another burden perhaps, but small enough—a hallucination, maybe an image out of his guilt about his sordidness. A price to pay, he thought, meager for what he received in return.

If that was all to it he was a fortunate man, he thought. Think of those stricken and suffering and unable to walk or play a piano for sins that destroyed them, starting in the mind.

He thankfully enlisted for life in the company of whores and their customers.

EIGHT

Remember Me to Katie

Tom left the empty funeral parlor. Whatever the final word was between them, it had been said. Good-bye, Con, now that all's said and done.

Spring, even with death in it, held a special bite of cool air and promise and an ache for what wasn't going to happen this time either. The May air outside Haggerty's Funeral Home was less than frosty. The lights from the Irish Club upstairs on the second floor at Oakland Avenue were so pale and reticent as they fell on the sidewalks that Tom Plower, at the thought of such light and another spring, felt his heart would break.

Thomas had done well over the years. He had enough. If he could call back the ghosts of the boys he had put away hundreds of pitchers with upstairs he would have done that, only that, no more: a last word. It was always the same word: Was there no way to tell you our time was golden and I loved you?

He ascended the familiar three flights of stairs to the club. He had once run up the stairs as a boy of fourteen, seeking what life held above the street, but more, what life meant.

For all their years of talk, Thomas had never said enough to Katie or Con, her brother, about certain things. He nodded at the doorman who waved him in.

It had begun with Katie one summer day.

They had sat as children together in the back of a truck going out to South Park one St. Patrick's Day. She had sat across from him on a bench in the back of the truck. They were both nine.

That day he had swung at a softball and hit it far, and his father had clapped him on the back and said he was a strong kid. Katie bobbed and disappeared from his sight all day, and he did not remember Con being there in South Park at all. The children were allowed to sip at someone's beer occasionally. At night, as the adults' voices became louder, it felt good to be surrounded by his uncles and aunts. On the ride home the children stretched out on the flatbed of the truck; Katie slept and he slept next to her. He heard her breathing and the sounds of his family in the cab of the truck, shouting out songs and wishing passers-by on the sidewalk, "Happy St. Patrick's Day."

As streetlights flickered on her face, the truck passing into circles of light, then shadow, he thought her the greatest beauty he had ever seen and wondered if this was love he felt.

She stayed in his mind, and he never spoke to her, seeing her in school, at the Irish Club on a certain holiday, Con's sister. He wondered if she saw him watching her and wishing the building would catch fire and he could save her. Against the purity of his devotion, complexity began its contamination one day when he was sixteen.

When Plower told Con he was in love with Katie, Con said nothing at first. A week later, Con asked, "Were you serious in what you said about Katie?"

Plower said, "Yes, I'm going to ask her to go to a movie with me."

"Over my dead body," Con said. "I'll break your jaw you fool with her."

They had played basketball together on the court at St. Agnes and in high school, Con the superior by far; Plower hadn't made the team. They had spent days sitting together on the stone steps to Joyce's Pharmacy and laughing at all the jokes in the air from the other boys, but they had had a secret laugh and nudge for each other later. They had followed together girls from the Mount Mercy Academy on Terrace Street, which cut across Robinson and Dunseith, and had been rebuffed together. They usually wandered home at dawn from the Irish Club, stopping halfway up the hill to clarify matters unstated or misunderstood earlier. After, the sun came up on the Presbyterian Hospital as they stood near home and the morning light cast shadows created by the large hospital looming over them. Plower thought it would be inevitable that he and Katie should love each other and one day marry. They would all go on this way forever.

"What did I do?" Thomas indignantly asked Con, not sure his friend wasn't pulling his leg. "Do you think I'm one of those guys who would misuse a girl? Con, I'm not the worst of guys."

"I know things," Con said. "Drop the subject."

"I don't know much more about things than Katie—I'm not going to kid you."

"Stay away!" Con said, no answers in his sullen silence.

If he looked in the mirror at the Irish Club, would Con be there on the next stool?

He stayed away from Katie, except for one other time.

"Good morning," he said one day as he passed her on Forbes when they were eighteen.

She turned to look at him with—he could be mistaken—abject confusion.

"She told me you spoke, and I asked you to stay away," Con said. "I warned you because she's strange. She meant you more trouble than you did her."

They sat on the wall of the Mount Mercy Academy, watching the girls. "I find her beautiful," Thomas said, not caring. Con was capable of crashing someone with his big fists for small provocation.

"She'll do," Con said, "but she ain't normal."

"That's a brother talking."

Con was silent. He slid off the stone fence. "Let's stroll after that one," he said. "Maybe she'll lose her senses and fall into bed with one of us." They followed a girl in the dark blue academy uniform, but she was that afternoon as unaware of them as she was that it was another day touched with gilt and sun and it was passing too quickly.

"Captain Blood," Thomas said before they parted, "remember me to Katie."

Katie became fat and peculiar. Thomas saw her at a distance at Mass.

She developed over the years into a huge shadow of her stout mother. The two women ate boxes of chocolate together, and Con supported them with a job he held as an auto mechanic. Thomas took on work as a bartender after high school for a man named Pates, and when Pates became ill when Thomas was near thirty, Pates's wife made Thomas a partner.

When the former owner died, the widow sold the bar to Thomas. At thirty he owned a quiet neighborhood bar in East Liberty that netted him thirty-six thousand a year, a good sum in 1958. He called the bar "Plower's." He married a woman he had known from Oakland, a widow with two children, and had two children with her.

He occasionally met with Con, and they went upstairs to the Irish Club on a Saturday night but did not talk as they once did until the morning sun rose over the rooftops in Oakland. Con seemed old; he was not cut out to be an auto mechanic. He drank more than he talked. He married, and his wife left him and he did not marry again. He lived with his mother and sister on Robinson.

They spoke of Katie once.

Con said, "She's a recluse. She doesn't leave the house except to go to church. She sits upstairs with the mother and the two of them say two words to each other in an hour. It's spooky. They turn on the television, but they turn down the sound. They sit there as if they're talking, but they ain't. I come home my voice is the only voice in the house. Sometimes I don't hear another voice until I go back to the shop."

"Con," Thomas had said, "it was love. I was young: it wasn't like my heart was shattered. It was that you didn't want me that hurt worse than losing Katie."

That was as close as he came to saying that sixteen had been perhaps his only time for love and he would never know its like again. He loved his wife, he loved his children; but, sixteen—it was when love and want ran like a poison in the bloodstream and destroyed everything before it. I've had fun, Thomas thought, the night of the funeral, but back then it was like cyanide and it felled me with its force.

He finished his drink and walked down well-known streets to Robinson. He hungered for a last word.

Con's mother let him in, and he saw Katie. She sat like a statue carved in massive stone. Her hair was as white as her mother's and her face beneath it was couched in folds of flesh that almost obscured her face. Thomas blinked. Could he remember the girl who had once moved about with the grace of an aimless starling?

Her arms lay at her sides like cruel slabs, her hands in her lap inert and helpless. She did not look at him as he stood watching her. She did not seem to recognize him. He put his hand to his hair. He remembered her one night at the Irish Club. She had twirled on the floor like a thistle caught in contrary winds. She had stomped the floor in her delicate black patent shoes. She had dashed her beautiful head about until he had become dizzy watching her.

Maybe all the underaged boys who drank beer there, guests of their parents and uncles and aunts at fourteen on the grand holidays, then graduating to regulars at sixteen, felt that particular call in the blood where spring and drink confused rational thought.

They entered as children, put on years, bristles, wrinkles, and emerged on other spring evenings decades later accomplished drunkards. To say "I knew him as a boy" was to say nothing at the Ancient Order of Hibernians (although it was said once an hour about someone).

Anyone who knew any of the attendant Irish Club veterans on any night knew them as a boy.

Sometimes, Thomas remembered, there with Con's mother and Katie, someone reared back on his chair at the Irish Club, tilted his face up to the overhead fan, and screamed with Celtic pleasure and thirst to drink down the night too. And barely anyone turned to look, but understood. Sometimes, wordlessly, four boys at midnight in May, Thomas and Con among them, ran down the two flights of stairs from the Ancient Order of Hibernians, Local No. 9, to Oakland Avenue, thundered in a pack out to the statue of Honus Wagner outside Forbes Field, where they veered again. They ran into Schenley Park and did chin-ups under the old trees at midnight or rolled down Flagstaff Hill in somersaults or curved in on themselves like babies waiting to be born. Grass-stained and wet from the water Thomas and Con had thrown on each other from the park's fountains, they walked slowly back to the Irish Club, not satisfied, but quieted.

Thomas felt strangled by the gloom in the air. It was, after all, spring outside. If he ran now, he would collapse after a block or two. He would not run.

Thomas stood uncertain and walked slowly toward Katie and her mother.

"I hope you're well as can be," he said generally to both women, and neither looked up, but the mother at the floor, the other across the room. "I'm Thomas Plower," he said, "a boyhood friend of Con's, do you remember?"

Katie's white hair lay tossed on her head. Had he seen her on the street, a stranger, he would have looked away. Her eyes were wild.

"I don't guess you remember me well," he said, starting to back away. It had been more than thirty years since she had glared at him one afternoon in Oakland, at his greeting to her then.

She turned and stared directly into his eyes. "I remember you," she said, her voice thick with rage. "You had that one thing on your mind about me and I see it in your face now. You ain't changed a bit. You filthy thing! Can't you leave me in peace? I can't bear the sight of you."

Katie took her mother's hand for comfort and retreated back to where the girl lived who once, light as a flock of birds in flight, could rest in a body on a high ribbon of cord and never by a motion cause the slightest quiver in the wire.

On the porch in the crisp air, Con's mother said, "She didn't mean a word she said. She has you mixed up with another friend of Con's."

She was still sturdy, reassuring as she took his arm. "There's a chance here," she said.

"No," he said. "You don't understand."

"Between what Con left us and my late husband there's forty thousand dollars."

Thomas shook his head. The cool air and other springs mocked him.

"Don't give me that," the woman said, "I see it in your eyes. Do it." She paused. "Do it, you hear? It's more money than you'll ever see in one piece in your life."

"I'm married," Tom said.

"Don't lie, Con's listening."

"He knows I'm telling the truth."

"Then why'd you come? Not for me. You came for her, right?"

"I came in respect for Con."

Her fingers were deep in his arm. "Do it," she said. "I'll talk to her. You can have her now. She's all yours."

He took her hand away as gently as he could. "No, good-bye."

"Why'd you come?" the old lady shouted after him, and Tom walked faster down the hill to avoid scandal.

In the dark park and on Robinson, he and the rest had run in pursuit of completions when the answer already lay in their panting throats, their eyes wet with chase, their tongues dry with expectations. The race was it; and that was over. Age brought not wisdom: or, Tom thought, it visited on a simple saloon-keeper the wrong truths.

Tears lay heavy on his face as he walked down the street to St. Agnes and the cab home. He wept softly because, he thought, taken all in all, the bunch of us are dead as Con, and no flower growing in May can revive us to what we used to be.

PART FOUR

Boys in the Age of Miracles

NINE

The Madonna of the Jukebox

ON THE night of January 8, 1945, at about ten minutes after eleven o'clock, a figure, a face really, appeared on the wall to the right of the jukebox at the Ancient Order of Hibernians, Local No. 9. The wall was of a greenish gray cast, and the figure, a sort of woman with a shawl covering her head, had in her outlines the same colors that the jukebox threw. The figure was a pale orange, like a tangerine too long in the sun, green in certain lines of her shawl. Where the eyes should have been in a drawing it was dark and obscure. The eyes of the figure were an artful representation. They were blank.

Rubber Hughes saw it first. "Mark," he said, standing in his lop-sided fashion and pointing: "It's the Holy Mother."

After several people sitting at the table insisted they saw nothing—they had all of them, after all, been sitting over their pitchers of beer since six—there was general agreement that an apparition had appeared on the wall near the jukebox.

Terrence Coleman, who had been one of the first to be drafted, had gone to Italy with General Clarke, lost two fingers, and was one of the first to return to Oakland, said, "It's the colors of the jukebox, lads. You're witnessing a reflection from the music box."

But a quick test by Cleet Cavanaugh established a mystery. He ran his hand in an arc between the jukebox and the wall. There was

107

no shadow on the wall from his hand. Such light as fell from the jukebox was not reaching the wall at that point where the figure lay. There were other lights from the jukebox cast on the wall and floors. One could cause them to change by running one's hand between the jukebox and them. But this configuration of shadows, lines, colors, and form sat by itself, unfazed by the gyrations of the men who tested the apparition on the wall. It was established, though, by a march across the long hall, through curious onlookers at other tables, that there were certain lights from the jukebox that fell the length of the place with no seeming connection to the Wurlitzer. A chair, it was observed, some two hundred feet away held the same distinct orange as the figure on the wall, and no amount of arm waving could cause the colors to recede or vanish. It was agreed the illusions of light in the club were profound in their mysterious patterns; but that still did not explain—even if light played crazy tricks—why its formations had decided to become, however accidentally, the figure of a very sad woman on the Irish Club wall on January 8, 1945.

There were perhaps forty resident drinkers in the club that night, in a cold winter, and when the word went out among them that a figure had appeared on the wall, people pulled their chairs into a semicircle and sat looking at the image. It was as if they expected it to move or speak to them. But at dawn, when the last witness had left and Paul Kerry, the manager, locked the door, the figure had neither indicated it was anything religious nor any interest in the club beyond being there.

I had the flu that first day and was not able to attend the arrival of the apparition. I came to the club four days after the figure had appeared.

Then I was greeted as I walked in by Pal Mahoney, who had with Cleet, Shadow Dully, Rubber Hughes, Terrence Coleman, Brian Smith, Denis Prior, and Dickie Trent what amounted to ringside seats for the spirit on the wall. They had pushed their tables together.

"I'm pleased," Pal said, waving me toward the table in his cordial manner and pushing over to me an Iron City that had been sitting before him, "to have an atheist in our midst tonight for a genuine reading of our situation."

Having played this game virtually since boyhood with Pal, I did not say, "I am a Jew, Pal, I am not an atheist." Because then Pal would have said, "And do they truly believe in God, Clifton?" and when I'd answer, "Of course," he'd say, "But not Jesus Christ. They say, I understand, He is not God." He'd shake his large head and say, "It's a strange religion, that one, but I respect it, you understand. I'm sure God has His purposes for it."

So rather than begin our old litany, I said, "I'm pleased to be here in whatever auspices I'm welcomed."

"Jesus Christ, Pal," Brian Smith said, "this is Clifton, this ain't a Jew. It's Clifton from up on Robinson."

Brian later lost a leg in Korea, and I strolled with him the week of his return to Oakland out to the statue of Stephen Collins Foster at the entrance to the Carnegie Museum. He said, "I'd like to bomb that statue," and I asked, "Why?" But he didn't answer my question directly. "And I'd like to bomb the museum," Brian said, "and the library and burn all the books. Then I'd like to shoot my mother and General MacArthur and you and then myself," and I understood the answer to my question.

"How're you feeling?" Denis Prior asked with great concern. Prior, in apparently robust health, was, the joke went, susceptible to other people's symptoms.

"Fine," I said, "fine, except I had the chills."

"It's cold out," Pal said, "it's terribly cold out, and it isn't going to stop snowing until April."

It was a Saturday night in a bad cold and snowy day and rare: a ghost was among us in our warmth of being together. On a snowy day the coats and mackinaws at the club hung on the back seats of chairs to dry, puddles of melting snow forming on the wooden floor.

The coats smelled like wet dogs, and as the heat in the long hall rose with the dancers and the shouts and the sidestepping of drinkers lurching through the dancers to get to the bar, the Irish Club became hot to the skin of the face and hands, crept like an old friend under clothes to dwell next to the body. Smoke clung in the heat and it rested on the forehead and in the throat. Colors of the jukebox streamed across the room and reflected in the amber pitchers of beer. The feeling of a warm spot against the cold night outside contained color too. Heat had white beer bubbles in it; comfort lay in gray smoke occasionally driven before a fan, the scent of rain-soaked dog hair, floors wet with snow, and the spilled, acrid beer fumes that mingled with it: us and sights, sounds, and smells all together.

"What do you think of the apparition?" Dickie Trent asked. "Will you certify it a miracle?"

I saw what appeared to be a woman, downcast. Her face was thin and triangular. Other people in the club had arranged their tables so that the room was in tiers lined up with the figure on the wall at the center. "It's the figure of a woman," I said, "no mistake."

The talk was of spiritual things, no one venturing secular opinions about the war or the dearth of football at Pitt Stadium. "She comes in many forms," Shadow Dully said. "There's a rather famous story out of old China I'll pass on to you."

Shadow Dully woke at five every morning. He trotted as best he could—he was in his early sixties—down to St. Paul's Cathedral on Fifth. There, whatever priest he could find, he asked for his blessing. After picking up three or four from any priests available, he then hurried down Fifth to St. Agnes, where he accosted priests in the church or on the sidewalk and once more asked for their blessings. He could on a good day get seven or so blessings before most people in Oakland had their breakfasts. He had been doing it, it was said, for thirty years. When he was not performing odd jobs at his family's printing office, he hung about St. Agnes all day, listening to sermons, running errands for the priests. He fancied himself learned in Catholicism, and indeed he knew a great deal about affairs at the churches he frequented.

"About four hundred years before Christ was born," Dully said, "the Virgin appeared in China. Her father was an emperor over there, you see, and for one reason or another he had her head chopped off."

"Wait a minute," Brian said. "I never heard a story about China where someone didn't get their heads chopped off. Are you sure this story ain't some unverifiable fairy tale?"

"Well, I wasn't there! But my source is a good one—oh, a very good one." Shadow put on a sober face, closed his eyes, and nodded. "I might say to you it came to me from higher than a priest, if you know what I mean."

"The Vatican?" Cleet asked.

"No, it wasn't out of the Sistine Chapel, but I mean no disrespect when I say to you I would accept this fellow's word as good as that of his Holiness himself."

"They chopped off her head," Pal Mahoney said. "Could you go on, Shadow; the Last Judgment ain't that long in coming."

"Well, she turned down the option of going to heaven," Shadow said. "It was offered her. But, no, she says, 'As long as there's people in hell I'm not going to heaven.' She says this, mind you, while she's down there: she's down there in hell with all the devils plaguing her and doing torment to her, and she says, 'I'm not moving a foot until you release some of these damned souls from hell!' The upshot of the matter was that the devil himself begged her to leave, promised, as they say, to pay her way out. But, no, she won't budge an inch. Finally, the Holy Spirit came, and He says, 'All right, you made your point. Maybe we're too hard on some of those people in hell, but you know they brought it on themselves. Just come along now: I'll do what I can.' And she says, 'No, Sir, not until you clear out the whole mess of them. As long as there's one person in hell, I'm not setting foot in heaven.' Right this minute there's a shrine to her off the coast of China; but, of course, they don't call her the Virgin Mary. They have their name for her, but that's who she is—sure as that apparition there is her drawn on the wall like by a child with a crayon or two. She comes in one shape or another, one country or another, any time she pleases—you know, to make one of her points."

Pal Mahoney cleared his throat, a terrible time in a discussion. When he talked, it came usually out of a carburetor fueled with fires and flares picked up in Belgium when the Jesuits taught him to speak quickly enough that there might have been no thinking at all behind it. That preparation before he spoke: it meant Lawrence Mahoney had been at work on a contradiction and was growling in readiness. "Shadow, are you saying to all of us faithful sons," he asked, "including Clifton here, who has received an anointment from Richard Trent, that the Virgin Mary—dressed up as a China-woman—is standing somewhere between purgatory and heaven and not allowing the Lord to rest easy until He clears out hell of sinners? But before you answer, think over blasphemy: Are you saying the Virgin Mary isn't in heaven at this moment?"

Shadow looked about for support, and sensing none, settled the question on his own. "I haven't the head for such issues," he said. "I'm merely repeating a famous story told me by an ecclesiastical source."

"Have a little caution," Pal said, and patted my hand. "We have a young man innocent of religion here, and if we value his soul, we won't throw cold water on its flames by misinforming him. That scrawl on the wall is not the Holy Mother manifesting herself. It is a trick of something in the wall bleeding through, not human blood, mind, unless the Irish Club has heretics buried in the plaster—or it's the paint doing tricks. Or it's the plaster running—it might be rain that seeped down from the roof causing a configuration. One thing it ain't, it ain't our Lady."

Denis Prior, who had a long, thin neck, bobbed in his throat several times. "Maybe our Lady chose to come here to signify the end of the war," he said. "It's not impossible."

"The Germans broke through again," Brian Smith said. "Maybe they have a fearsome weapon and there's more coming. It might be a warning."

"She's sad," Shadow said. "She's come to tell us she's sad about the human lot."

It was too much for Pal Mahoney. He stood and said, "And you didn't know up till now the human lot made her sad? You needed to see her picture on the wall?" He left, throwing his coat over his shoulders, and Shadow said when he was gone, "She doesn't have to explain to Pal Mahoney why she came."

The next night it was decided—I was not there—that Denis Prior would go down to Father Farrell at St. Agnes and tactfully, very discreetly, like a man walking in a minefield, explain that some of his parishioners would appreciate it if he came for five minutes up to the Irish Club and looked at what some superstitious fools were claiming was a ghostly appearance. I was there, seated before the apparition, when Denis brought back Father Farrell's reply. "He said to me to remember his every word," Denis said. "He said, 'Put me down on the record, son. I don't want my immortal words to be lost in the translation: If the misfits up at the Irish Club drink enough beer, it wouldn't surprise me if they saw Rhett Butler and Scarlett O'Hara and the burning of Atlanta on the wall up there!'" Denis looked about to all of us. "That was his message."

Shadow shook his head. "You wouldn't think a priest would have anything but an open mind on some subjects," he said. "I'll speak to Father the next time I see him. It ain't scientific to maintain such an attitude."

The next day Rubber, who was called by that name because of an arthritic spine that had bent him over since youth, claimed he felt fit and better than he had in years. To those who went down to visit him in his house on Bates Street, where he lived with his sister, he said, "I was the first person to see the figure, you remember?" While he was not dancing about, Terrence, Denis, a boy named Bob Greeley, who had an interest in the occult, and Brian all said he did seem a little more erect. He walked about for them, even did a dance step or two.

Pal Mahoney, at the Irish Club, waved it away. "I've seen him jig here on many St. Patrick's Days," he said, "and he always says the same thing: 'I do believe I'm restored.' I put no stock in it."

Denis Prior was again sent to St. Agnes, this time to speak to Father Rainer, a new priest who had been there a year, and to request of him that he join certain Catholic youth in a friendly drink the following Sunday night. "He says to me," Denis said, when he returned, "'I know your intention, Denis, and my word on the subject is this: I don't need to see God on the wall of the Irish Club, or His mother either. He's somewhere there in every human face I'm privileged to see from sunup to sundown.' That's what the young fellow said to me."

Pal Mahoney said, "Well, does that settle the matter?"

Most, still watching the apparition from the edge of their eyes, did not know what to make of it, not certain as the priests or Mahoney were but not embracing the supernatural as Rubber and Shadow had.

In the midst of what was a quiet moment—a sort of truce of beer and even a lengthy reference to the declining fortunes of the wartime Pittsburgh Steelers, unhappily merged with Philadelphia—a boy named Larson approached the table and asked Terrence Coleman to lend him a dollar.

Pal struck his forehead. "She's come for him!" he cried, pointing at Larson, who was called for sound reasons even as a child Grand Larson.

Larson had recently appeared at the Irish Club and in Oakland with what seemed thousands of streetcar tokens. The tokens normally sold three for a quarter, and one could take a passenger all the way across Pittsburgh. Larson sold the tokens five for a quarter, and people, believing that Larson had devised some scheme to defraud the Pittsburgh Railways, bought the tokens eagerly. But it developed Larson had broken into the lockers of one of the nuns who taught at the Mount Mercy Academy on Terrace Street and stolen her prudent fund of streetcar tokens. The tokens felt contaminated after that.

"Here's this nun," Mahoney said, standing to his full length. "She knows the world is coming to an end—it's her vocation—and all she can think of is to store away a few streetcar tokens. You see, it's how she's being practical, coping, you know, with the temporal. You never know how at the time of the Second Coming someone might not need a streetcar fare to get out to East Liberty, where the Lord is going to appear, or downtown. I do not profess to know the mind of a nun. And this fellow steals what is probably her only worldly possessions. Now, I ask this question of everyone at the table: Who has the apparition come to this club to save if it ain't Mr. Bernard Larson, known as Grand?"

Larson asked, "Why are you picking on me, Pal? I didn't ask you for no loan."

"There have been conjectures here," Mahoney said, "that a vision has descended on us and that it has to do with the horrors of war, the sufferings of mankind—but the question was always, Why here? And the answer is: Because Grand Larson walks these boards and the Little Sport and their friend Chokey Samuels, who last week stole a police car from in front of the Number 4 Oakland Police Station."

"I never bother anybody," Larson said, backing away.

"She's come to get you," Mahoney called across the room.

Safe at a table miles away from Mahoney, Larson shouted back, "Go to hell, Mahoney, the Jesuits cracked your brain."

"Hey, Mahoney," the Little Sport, who was at the table with Larson and had done everything lately except steal a nun's tokens, called, "She come for you, except you're too fat."

The next day the image was gone. If one peered at where it had been from certain angles, it was obvious it had been painted over. "Who'd have done that?" Brian asked, and Terrence said, "Maybe the same supernatural force that put it there in the first place. It don't have to use magic all the time: it can use paint and enamel if that's its wish."

Denis Prior said, "The whole thing gave me a nervous stomach. I liked the place before the miracles started."

"It wasn't no miracle," Cleet said.

"The whole thing gave me headaches," Denis said.

Paul Kerry, the manager and bartender at the Ancient Order of Hibernians, Local No. 9, told me a few years later that it was he who had painted over the apparition. "Weren't you sort of afraid?" I asked.

"If the image didn't like it, she could always come back through the paint or have the roof of the club blow away in a hurricane, or drown Pittsburgh under thirty feet of water," he said. "I got tired of rearranging those chairs and tables every night as if I were running a cabaret."

A person, I thought, makes the choice of his own miracles: for me, at the core of magic—larger in memory than the embracing odors of old perfume and overcoats and the seductive color of cigarette smoke as it evaporates to white—was the music of our talk. Before the last year of the war was out, Paul and Terrence and I were pallbearers at Denis Prior's funeral. The boy, seventeen at the time, died in his sleep as if he were a little old man rather than a noisy youth. He saw no surrender in Europe in May, no atom bomb in August, went on no further pilgrimages to the clergy to clarify ghostly appearances at the Irish Club. He sleeps where there are none of our mysteries, or our voices either.

TEN

Grady's Sister

A LIGHT RAIN had fallen on Forbes. The air was cool. The lights in all the shops were particularly bright as evening fell. Spring lay thin and fine on the bright bars and shafts that the neon lights struck on the sidewalks. On Anna Marie's night, the sound of trolleys climbed the old stone buildings and bounced off the chimneys.

The talk of Grady's sister fell like the April mist settling in among the telephone poles, the streetcar tracks, the small knots of young men who gathered at their customary corners and stores. Anna Marie was more real than the cool night or the soft breeze, more a plan for the night than *Rebecca* at the Strand Theater. The excitement may have been there that something was ending in Oakland.

Grady's sister, Anna Marie, a young woman of seventeen who had been hidden away from the streets of Oakland for most of her life, had recently come to Forbes Street with the fanfare due a New York debutante arriving at the Stork Club. She plainly had no sense of how to act. She came across naked and free to anyone who'd ask, sinking after a few weeks into the combined hands of the Big Sport, Hands O'Malley, the Little Sport, Sharkie Manly, and Bingo Dornegan, a somewhat older man in his early thirties.

The girl had apparently once planned to be a nun, her father a respectable policeman for twenty years, the brothers all steadily working, and Grady DeForrest himself the assistant manager at the fountain at the big Isalys on the boulevard. Somewhere between the brothers and father sheltering her—the policeman was a widower— she had misunderstood herself. She had read of love in *Photoplay* and *True Confessions* and thought the boys who accumulated around her where she walked or stopped for a soda at the Sun Drug were characters played in movies by Van Heflin or Robert Taylor. When one asked, she agreed, then another, and another. She saw no reason to draw the line on two or three at a time—or ten—until she appeared again in Oakland on the spectacular evening in April 1941 that tried Dick Best's soul.

He had been friends with Grady since both had attended St. Agnes from the first grade on. They had acted together every year in the annual Christmas pageant. Not that Dick had liked Grady. Grady had a low forehead and hair that grew red and spiky two inches above his fair eyebrows. He had a short nose and was generally calm but erupted once a year in quick fury on anyone who provoked him. It didn't take much. No one knew what triggered his rages. It could be a word or a look. He'd whirl, put his head down, and seize someone by the shirt or collar and thrust them against the nearest wall.

If Grady hadn't already smashed the person in the face, it usually took two people, or three, to pry Grady loose from his victim. His fingers would lock on the cloth, his face frozen in unexplainable rage. The nuns pried his fingers loose one by one from someone's collar, his eyes bulging. Fortunately for Dick Best, who was considered Grady's best friend but feared him like everyone else did, Grady's rages weren't frequent. But someone seeing one would never forget it. Dick Best avoided him, but Grady, who had moments of softness as inexplicable as his angers, followed Dick about over the years and talked about Shelley and Keats. He asked Dick if he expected Shelley would ever get to heaven, how long would purgatory last for Voltaire, and did Dick believe that Grady's mother, dead when the boy was ten, was with them that very minute. It seemed Grady was always around. Wherever Dick turned, Grady would be there. He went to every football game in Oakland or stood around on corners. Until the family moved, Dick expected to see Grady any night he went down into Oakland. He set up free milkshakes and sundaes when Dick came into the dairy store and often asked him to go out to the Oval and catch a football on Sunday. Torn between friendship and his madness for women, it was hard then for Dick to make a decision about Grady's sister, Anna Marie, the night she went to the Strand Bowling Alley, upstairs from the movie theater, and set records for a woman not knowing the score. Thinking it over, hearing the talk all night, Dick Best decided it was friendship that counted, even if Grady wasn't the ordinary sort of friend.

The talk about Grady's sister hurried down Forbes, up the alleys, and around to the Irish Club, to the Sand Scratchers above Gammons, into the bars and drug stores. Wherever young men gathered that night—and some not so young, Bernie Salkoff, a soldier in the first war, Eddie McCurran, limping and no less than fifty—all went tumbling down to the Strand Bowling Alley. The bowling alley was usually closed after nine on Sundays, but Simon Murphy, who came in to clean up, had a key and let in Bingo Dornegan and the Little Sport with Anna Marie, and then word got out and the procession started. By the time Dick Best heard of the event, a line had formed at the bowling alley; down the stairs to the street and in twos and threes young men stood around on the sidewalk waiting their turn to climb the stairs and mount Anna Marie, who was lying upstairs on an old mattress Simmy slept on when he was through polishing the alleys. "There must be seventy-five guys in line," Tom Flannel told Dick about a quarter to one. "You'd better get over before the cops come or she decides she's had enough."

"They never do," said Glenn Leary. "There was one once out over the Luna Restaurant who did it for four days, rain and shine, stopping to have a bowl of soup and taking on the next guy."

"Well, you'd think," Dick Best said, "a person couldn't eat corned beef and cabbage for four days straight. Or drink free Iron City beer for four days. A person couldn't do anything for four days straight without something snapping." Dick had just tried a new hair cream, Brylcreem, on his coal black hair, and he rather thought it gave him a shine and a sparkle beyond Wildroot—a maybe winner's shot if he ran into something good that night—but with Anna Marie DeForrest upstairs from the Strand Theater, all the hair lotions in the world, the shoe polishes, the shoes themselves, for that matter, were of no importance at all in the whirl of capturing women. Anna Marie had what a fellow wanted; and she didn't require a dime, not a clean shirt even, no Hitchcock garters that held up a man's socks. It was unnatural. But it opened up possibilities in Dick that teased him, tormented him, pulled at him, and called him into worlds where he had only to part a thin curtain and there on the other side lay a universe upside down and inside out. It was a place not invented by nuns and priests. Buildings stood at forty-five-degree angles. There were no mothers there, or sisters—he had no sisters of his own anyhow—no well-dressed women on the street trailing perfumes, just Anna Marie somewhere, pure and simple, what a man wanted, no talk, no Brylcreem, no argyles, or Doublemint to cover up onions on a hamburger.

It was a violation of things in orderly place. It was an anarchy to all he understood. He was bothered by what Anna Marie was doing, but he did think it was something permissible if it happened only in the dark where only she knew it—and perhaps one other person. Then either could deny it happened—even to themselves—or one could accuse the other of exaggerating or even inventing the whole thing. One was best for sin: two was the outer limits. Not just the act of sex. But anything; there wasn't anything that happened, Dick thought, that shouldn't have enough secrecy or privacy to it that a person couldn't swear before the Supreme Court that not a word of it was true and expect fifty-fifty to be believed. Confession before Father Farrell was fair enough. You told him the sin, even answered questions about it, but the glowing mystery to it, the voluptuous reaches of it going beyond the recitation of facts, lay hidden to boil again in the recesses of the imagination. But the unnatural lay about Anna Marie on Simmy's mattress upstairs at the Strand because of the long line of men who could now testify about the deed before the world, leaving Anna Marie no room to dance herself free of the sin by lying.

Perhaps she was of such a mind she did not think it a dark deed. Puzzling it, Dick Best thought it rose in the air all about him like sweet perfume given form. Nothing prosaic or less than sin ever had that sweep of promise and forbidden expectation, a fullness, a completion. And thinking of Anna Marie, whom he had seen about since she was a child, she soared in his imagination on Forbes. She stirred him to a longing such as he had never known, and with the yearning a contract that the longing could be eased by the girl upstairs at the Strand. She lingered beautifully in the thin April air about him. Her hair flowed like streams of swallows. Her arms were white and long, and he had to blink her away before she caused his mind to fail altogether at rational thought. It was the opportunity of a lifetime. She would have more than a hundred men that night in Oakland, and she'd hardly remember to speak to anyone of Dick Best, if she ever spoke of the subject at all. Pulling up his collar against the wind, hot with expectation, he went to stand in line.

The men joked. The DeForrest family had been gone from Oakland for five years, and no one saw the brothers on the streets. "Weren't you a friend of Grady's?" Bob Gray asked Dick, two men in front of him.

"I knew him," Dick said. "We went to school."

"He's got to know something of this," Eddie Toony said.

A thin, dark boy named Zungo said from under formidable black brows, "He can't. He'd have to kill. I'd find every guy connected with it if it was my sister and I'd put every one of them to the ice pick. Find out every one of them and cut them apart."

"Man, I'm glad it ain't your sister," Bob Gray said.

Behind them, two other men, older, fell in to line. "Twice for me," one of them said. "I was here two hours ago."

"I bet there's a lot in this line been up more than once," the other man said.

Bob Gray said, "I think that's a man's own business."

"Hey!" one of the older men called. "I'll give a fiver to any of you up the top of the stairs give me his place."

"Make it fifty," someone called down.

"Fifty," Gray said to Dick Best. "That's not Betty Grable up there."

The line extended up the stairs, young men leaning on the wall, some hands in their pockets moving up slowly, a minute or two at a time. Watching the old faces he had known since boyhood, Dick was struck by a singular omission. A gathering this large—it might have been the annual Oakland Community–Irish Club football game on Thanksgiving—would surely once have held the short, powerful figure of Grady DeForrest. Scowling under his thick red hair, trying to look connected to the moment—laughing if someone else did, serious if the talk turned complex—Grady, hands in pockets, would be there. Dick found himself looking for Grady, knowing that of all the young men who could have been in the line to savor Anna Marie—strangers from the South Side who had somehow heard and miraculously appeared at the Strand, visitors from out in East Liberty, pool hustlers who had interrupted their game down in Soho at the news—old Grady, the born hanger-on, could not be there.

Anna Marie had banished him.

She had peculiarly caused him to share her sin, and Dick Best felt a cold chill. Me too, he thought; she's run me into absence with her brother.

He was taken with a terrible vision—but not of anything he could see; instead, a spectacle of emptiness in the long line. It was a line that could hold all the young men in the world he had ever known, except one. The vision was of a man without edges, faceless and voiceless. Grady was excluded.

It was shadows marked by the worst thing that could swim before a person's eyes, Dick thought: emptiness. It was a world without fullness and a promise of a future. Those men in line, Anna Marie, a thousand daisies all different in some microscopic way, all would be swallowed by that blank dissolution where poor Grady and Anna Marie were now. Dick Best, who believed in friendship, shuddered at the point in the line where red-haired Grady should have stood. She had wrapped Dick into the public nature of her conduct with her brother.

Anna Marie and I are a pair, he thought, causing a void to be set down on a Sunday night on Oakland. Exclusion from things: there's no sin worse, he thought, and I was standing about pleased with my jolly fornication.

He fell back from the line, joining Grady, who now had company, not the only man forbidden from the long line to his sister.

"Where you going?" Zungo asked.

"Grady's a friend of mine," Dick Best said bravely before the universe, not liking Grady and his mad rages one inch more than he had.

"I respect that," Bob Gray said.

"Damn it all," Dick said, not wanting to make any more a fool of himself than he had, probably famous now as the youth who wouldn't climb the stairs to Anna Marie. But the dark street he saw as he stood out on Forbes was crowded with all the wonders that made for jumbled-up life. Nothing out here was shut out. Cars, trees, trailers clanging, and nowhere he looked under red skies was the awful shadow of nothing there.

The corner poles with their swaying streetlights in the gray morning were real with a light that fell their length. The sidewalks rang with his footsteps. He never expected to feel so right again. He loved Grady's sister at that moment.

Near the corner of Craft and Forbes he saw a woman who could only be Grady's mother climbing the stairs to the Juvenile Detention Hall. She carried a shopping bag. She was going to work to clean the offices.

Dick ran up the steps after the woman. He could not let her climb the stairs with the heavy shopping bag.

But the woman was nothing like Grady's mother up close. She was shorter, stouter. What had he been thinking of?

The woman stepped back, startled; she held her bag close. Smart woman. She thought him a thief come to snatch her pathetic bag with its rags and sponges.

"Sorry," he said, retreating.

He tried to get back his feeling of love for miserable Grady and his sister. A feeling of rightness.

No, it was just the old Grady again in his mind and his real-life sister and the woman wasn't his mother, to be helped a final few steps with her bag. Nothing but morning light now and nothing there to recapture last night's springtime wonder of a woman veiled in ardor and mischief, ease in a complicated life.

ELEVEN

The Road to Damascus

"THE TOUGHEST thing of all," Ned Durgan said, "is to find a place to take a girl once you find one who will go anywhere at all with you. A fellow could rent a room in a hotel downtown, but that'd cost twenty dollars before you're through, and there's house detectives and your old aunt that hasn't been in the Earle Hotel downtown in forty years and she stepped in with Father Farrell to observe a chandelier from when she was first married and the hotel was respectable, and there you are tucking your shirt in your pants with a girl with lipstick on her cheek and your reputation is in tatters."

"What's someone to do?" Biff Chambers asked. "You can't be running girls to the park like when we were twelve or hiding in doorways. We're all in our twenties now."

Pal Mahoney said, "Just follow what you've been taught and keep your pants zipped. Did anyone ever get in trouble following St. Paul? There wasn't any syphilis on the road to Damascus, Ned, and there wasn't gonorrhea. No one had the shame of bringing a girl to pregnancy and then taking a stroll down to the corner cigar store and saying, 'I was out of town that weekend.'"

Ned Durgan and Pal Mahoney had both been altar boys at St. Agnes and both had planned to be priests. Durgan's oldest brother, John, had in fact become a priest, the first on Robinson Street, and

Mahoney, an only child, had decided early to make his mother and father proud and join the clergy. But Ned had gone off to become one of the most successful skirt chasers in the history of the Irish Club, and Pal Mahoney, with no recognizable sins anyone could summon up easily, hadn't found women distracting him from the priesthood but, I suspect, the Roman Catholic Church itself, not subtle enough to meet his perceptions of right and wrong and men and women. I asked, "What's your solution, Ned?"

Berry Flynn, who was at the table and had been there first some five pitchers of beer and four hours earlier, said, "These subjects have a limited interest to you, Clifton, being Jewish. Your people have another standard. Jews can take a girl to their mother's room and no one will shout recriminations. There's no confession and no scandal. You're the luckiest people on the planet and that's why you preen yourselves as the chosen people. You damn well are. Sex is something you do like sneezing, no mere sense of guilt about it."

"No, you're wrong," Ned said. "They're worse than we are. I know what I'm talking about. When they get started—mind, it has to be a subject that catches their fancy—they could give the College of Cardinals lessons in how to befuddle a suffering humanity. Do this, do that. And I don't think you should hold poor Clifton there responsible for the sins of a people: whatever philosophy the poor boy abides by, I don't see him doing any better at the skin game than the average fellow here in the Irish Club."

"I appreciate your acknowledgment that I'm a failure, Ned," I said.

Berry Flynn said, "I was only speaking generally, Clifton; I wasn't intending anything personal. You know there isn't a person here wouldn't jump into a fire for you. Well, maybe old McGrath at the door, but you know what I mean."

Pal laughed. "Being Irish," he said, "we'd hit that fire for you before we'd do it for each other."

"This is a serious subject," Ned said, "and I think I should clarify the position of the Jewish people on sex." He waited to see if there were any objections, and Cleet came in the door, and Berry Flynn waved at him. "Rege," he called, "Ned's going to tell us about race and sex. Don't miss a word."

Cleet brought a pitcher of beer and nodded all around and sat at the table.

"Well, I was seeing a girl," Ned said, "not from this neighborhood so don't anyone get mad at me. She was Irish, I confess, but I never said I was strong." He lit a cigarette and inhaled slowly. The dark lashes on his blue eyes fell as he went back over the girl. "Yes," he said, as if someone had asked, "she was a beauty, the darling looking more like fifteen than twenty, which was her age. I met her when I was out delivering flowers for Leonard's at Easter. I brought this bouquet of mums up to the door of a mansion out in Squirrel Hill, and to the door comes this Irish angel. Now, it's important that you remember she looked years younger than her legal age, which was two months short of twenty-one. I almost dropped the flowers. I said, 'You're not the lady of the house?' and she said, 'I'm not the lady of anything. I just work here on weekends.' Well, she's the daughter of a retired coal miner out in Castle Shannon and her name is Deirdre, and we hit it off from the second we met. I might have been bringing her that basket of mums personally she was so pleased with me. We struck it off famously and I was kissing her in an hour, and in the next half hour she swore she'd love me forever."

"It's the part about the Jews I'm interested in," Pal said. "If this isn't an educational story, it's just Ned Durgan sailing out on the flying trapeze one more time. Right, fellows?"

"Let him tell it anyhow," Cleet said. "I don't need to be educated. Men with fourth-grade educations have a million in the bank."

"No," Ned said, "this isn't another did-well story."

"Go ahead," Berry said.

"Anyhow, I was stuck with where to take her," Ned said. He smiled his broad, white smile: one of four brothers, with the other two who weren't priests, famous lady-killers—smiles, blue eyes, and dark hair like shoe blackening but pale and broad-shouldered with long muscles, although none of them held jobs requiring strength. "I went over it in my mind and Deirdre tried to help," Ned said. "She wasn't, you understand, a shy girl. Not that she was fast; she just was straightforward. We had business before us and I guess it was the coal miner's mentality there: no way to get at the rock but to lift up the pick and shovel and go at it. The house was no place; the lady might be home any hour and she needed the job bad. Desperate, I could walk her into a hotel on the North Side, but I'd have been arrested for luring away a kid from her confirmation. So I did what any reasonable person does: I called on my friends. I made contact with Tom Conroy, who was rooming out on Craig Street. Tom would never refuse me. 'I'll be out of this place at eight on Wednesday night,' he said, 'but I have a roommate, a fellow you might have seen around, Broomie Schneider.' 'Yes,' I said, 'I know Broomie. He went to Schenley with us. Will you give him my best?' 'I certainly will,' Tom said, 'and we'll be mice out of here before you arrive.'"

"Broomie Schneider is Jewish," Berry Flynn said. "I know him. He had a paper route down in Oakland. His father had a little cart where he sold hot cookies and nuts. His father had a name everyone called him, a Jewish name."

"*Mundele*," I said. "It means sesame seed."

Ned nodded. "It was Sesame Seed's son," he said. "He and Conroy were famous friends, went to the army together, roomed afterward, played cards with each other for years, inseparable friends until Tom got married last year. Well, I took Deirdre over there on Wednesday night, her night off, and I left her in the hall downstairs and went upstairs to the unlocked apartment, and there the two of them were, Broomie and Tom, playing cards. It was ten after eight and I don't know which one of them to this day engineered it to be there to see the girl. Can you imagine someone so squirrelly he hangs around just to see a girl who does?"

"I can imagine it," Cleet said. "Up to sixteen I'd have walked five miles just to see a girl who did."

"I'd have swum the Allegheny," Biff said.

"To me the impulse is very strange, since I imagined all women did sometimes," Ned said, "but that isn't the main point of my discussion, although I think something's wrong with young men who have nothing to do but pry—but I'll leave the subject. Anyhow, I said, 'Good evening, Broomie, good evening, Tom, I'm surprised to see you here.' They began shuffling cards and Broomie said, 'Where's the girl?' and I said, 'Downstairs. I didn't know what to expect up here. One of you might have been undressed or in bed. You might have at the last minute had a girl up here yourself. A big card game might have broken out with seven players, so I left the young lady downstairs until I scouted the lay of the land.'

"'You left her downstairs?' Broomie asked, standing. He wore thick glasses, you remember, and he studied me with them as if I were a bug under a microscope. 'I did,' I said. 'That's barbaric,' he said, and ran to the door. 'Wait,' I said 'what are you going to do?' 'Invite her up here,' he said. 'Broomie,' I said, 'this is none of your business. I'm borrowing your room, I'm not hiring you as my personal maître d'.' He put on a shirt and said, 'Let's go, Tom,' and they both stood and I thought I was rid of them. But walking downstairs, Broomie spotted Deirdre sitting off on a little bench near an umbrella stand—it wasn't a lobby at all, just a little square next to the front door—and he goes to her, puts out his hand, and says, 'I'm Broomie Schneider, pleased to meet you.' Deirdre, of course, put her hand out, and said, 'Deirdre Ryan.' Well, do you see it?"

"Nothing wrong so far," Pal Mahoney said, "except for the hanging around. But it could have been a mistake in time or an excessive interest in the card game. Then again, it could have been Conroy who instigated the impulse to hang around, so it'd prove nothing about the Jews generally."

"Broomie should have minded his own business," Berry said. "This wasn't his affair."

"Wait," Ned said. "The next day someone rang the doorbell to my house on Robinson at nine in the morning, and it was Broomie Schneider. It was bright outside so I went out on the porch and I said, 'Is there something wrong, Broomie?' I thought something was missing from the apartment: thoughts flashed through my mind about possibilities. 'Yes,' Broomie said, 'there's plenty wrong. Where do you get the nerve to debauch a young girl like that? Who gave you the right to degrade a sweet kid like Deirdre? To let her stand in the hallway like a woman you hired for the night? Even, Ned, to bring her to a place like Tom's and mine and expose her to influences you can't control. Does anyone know anyone else so well they can count on them in situations like that?' I was amazed. 'Broomie,' I said, 'I've known Tom all my life. You're a neighborhood guy. I wasn't bringing Deirdre into a den of thieves.' 'Not this time!' Broomie said. 'But I'm here to warn you, leave that girl alone. She's a sweet young kid. She's somebody's sister. Don't you have a heart?'"

Biff said, "It was none of his business."

"He meant well," Cleet said. "I don't blame him."

"Listen," Ned said. "Broomie pulled himself up right there on our front porch like a frog swelling, and he looked me in the eye and he asked, 'Are you going to marry Deirdre?'"

"None of his affair," Biff said.

Pal Mahoney said, "If I hadn't asked you the same questions, Ned, I'd have wanted to. Walking over bodies on the sidewalk isn't some people's style. Broomie saw something he disapproved of and he spoke. I think there's a golden streak in Sesame Seed's son. He saw wrong and he spoke out."

"I wish what I'm telling you ended here," Ned said. "But it didn't and I guess I'm partly to blame. The next Wednesday night I had the same problem. It's the toughest thing of all. There are fifty thousand women on the streets of Pittsburgh, but you can't walk into a hotel with one unless you expect to see your sixth-grade class from St. Agnes assembled for a reunion on the front stoop. I called Conroy again and he said, 'Sure,' and I went over to his place on Craig with Deirdre. This time the apartment was empty, and I left there about eleven at night.

"And there standing under a streetlight across from the boarding house is Broomie Schneider, as if he's merely waiting to return to his home and Deirdre and I are an afterthought. I tried to nod and move down Craig to catch a 68 streetcar out to Squirrel Hill, but Broomie came running across the street. He put his hand out and shook hands with Deirdre and me. Then he said, 'How is everyone?' and I said, 'Everyone is fine,' and tried to keep my momentum to Squirrel Hill. Understand, at this time I vowed I would die a monk in a Trappist monastery in St. Louis rather than come back to Craig Street—lust yes, a fool no. But it was too late. 'Do you realize what you're doing?' Broomie asked Deirdre. 'You're a sweet, young girl. One day you're going to have children like yourself. Are you going to want them if they're daughters to come out to places like this? You're too young to make decisions that'll stay with you forever.' And poor Deirdre—she's in tears—said, 'I'm almost twenty-one.' 'But you don't have a father here, there's no brother to protect you,' Broomie said. 'He shouldn't do this to you.' His eyes under those glasses, I'm telling you, were six inches across."

"What did you do?" Berry asked.

"I put my head down, took the girl by the elbow, and skulked down Craig as if I'd been caught stealing," Ned said.

"And the girl, Deirdre?" I asked.

"Clifton, who can face shame like that, out under a streetlight?" Ned asked. "Broomie might as well have been that coal miner father climbed up from the shaft to speak his piece. I was a victim of a maniac bad as Father Farrell at his worst. Father Farrell told me there are recorded cases of young men's noses falling off from unsavory habits. I was six then."

Biff laughed. "They used to say your ears would grow hair like a monkey's," he said.

"Don't tell me about a Catholic upbringing," Ned said. "I never saw Deirdre again. She slammed the phone down every time I called. Mind, she had no complaint with me. But Broomie raving under that streetlight on Craig had changed her life."

Pal Mahoney said, "He said what had to be said. Sesame Seed's son is the descendant of Isaiah and Jeremiah, you know. The world would be a better place if people looked into their Old Testament once a week instead of watching Milton Berle for the truth."

"Now, Clifton, don't take this wrong," Ned said, "but I know you well and I'd trip any Irishman who came at you on risk of my life. But my remark is addressed to Mr. Lawrence Mahoney: Pal, you should have been a Jew."

"I'd be honored," Pal said. "Up to a point, you understand."